'A collection of excellent essays…to be read by all who are interested in the spiritual dimension of professional counselling.'
    – *Elizabeth Ruth Obbard, Carmelite Nun, Author and Spiritual Director*

'Gubi's work, and that of his fellow writers, reminds us of the vital overlaps between psyche, spirit, mind, body and emotions, united in a life-giving task. This book provokes and enlivens by bringing together therapeutic and spiritual traditions in a creative dialogue.'
    – *Alistair Ross, Director of Psychodynamic Studies, University of Oxford*

also by Peter Madsen Gubi

Spiritual Accompaniment and Counselling
Journeying with Psyche and Soul
Edited by Peter Madsen Gubi
Foreword by Canon Professor Elaine Graham
ISBN 978 1 84905 480 5
eISBN 978 0 85700 861 9

Prayer in Counselling and Psychotherapy
Exploring a Hidden Meaningful Dimension
Peter Madsen Gubi
Foreword by Brian Thorne
ISBN 978 1 84310 519 0
eISBN 978 1 84642 751 0
Practical Theology Series

of related interest

The Psychology of Spirituality
An Introduction
Larry Culliford
ISBN 978 1 84905 004 3
eISBN 978 0 85700 491 8

Integrating Spirituality in Counseling
A Manual for Using the Experiential Focusing Method
Elfie Hinterkopf
ISBN 978 1 84905 796 7
eISBN 978 1 78450 083 2

What Counsellors and Spiritual Directors Can Learn from Each Other

Ethical Practice, Training and Supervision

Edited by PETER MADSEN GUBI

Jessica Kingsley *Publishers*
London and Philadelphia

First published in 2017
by Jessica Kingsley Publishers
73 Collier Street
London N1 9BE, UK
and
400 Market Street, Suite 400
Philadelphia, PA 19106, USA

www.jkp.com

Copyright © Peter Madsen Gubi 2017

Front cover image source: iStockphoto®

Library of Congress Cataloging in Publication Data
A CIP catalog record for this book is available from the Library of Congress

British Library Cataloguing in Publication Data
A CIP catalogue record for this book is available from the British Library

ISBN 978 1 78592 0 257
eISBN 978 1 78450 2 713

Printed and bound in Great Britain

This book is dedicated to

Dr W. Owen Cole, Revd Dr Derek Webster, Sr Teresa Duffy, Revd John Proctor, Professor Brian Thorne, Professor William West and Professor Neil Messer in gratitude for all that they have taught me.

Contents

Introduction

Peter Madsen Gubi

Discussions about the differences and similarities between counselling/ psychotherapy and spiritual accompaniment/direction abound in the published literature (e.g. Benner 2002; Gubi 2015a; Harborne 2012; Hart 2006; Leech 1994; Sperry 2003) and in workshops and seminars where therapists and spiritual directors meet for 'professional' development. Some say that they are very different 'disciplines', and others say that they are more similar than different. In my experience, it is usually those who are trained in one discipline, but not in the other, who accentuate the differences, rather than those who are trained in, and practise, both. Arguably, each discipline may have a vested interest in accentuating their difference, because to acknowledge the similarities has implications for training in both disciplines, and for the 'professionalisation' of spiritual accompaniment/direction, which some are against. Indeed, some may see it as a 'psychological captivity of the Church' (Jones 1995).

Although spiritual accompaniment/direction and counselling/ psychotherapy have had different historical and developmental journeys (see Harborne 2012, pp.16–23, for a fuller explanation of these developments), they both originated as a 'ministry to the soul'. 'Spiritual Direction is [a term] usually applied to the cure of souls' (Leech 1994, p.30), and the term 'psychotherapy' is derived from the Greek words *psyche*, meaning 'soul or breath of life', and *therapeia*, meaning 'attendant or servant' (West 2004, p.144). Arguably, spiritual direction has remained overtly truer to its purpose of soul-attending, depending on how the word 'soul' is defined. As counselling/psychotherapy has been professionalised and secularised, it has largely moved away from its spiritual antecedents (except for approaches to pastoral counselling and approaches to faith-based counselling) and has developed theory around a quasi-scientific psychological understanding of the psyche, with an anti-religious bias influenced largely by the writings of Freud (1961), in spite of the innately spiritual work of Jung (Goss 2015; Stevens 1994). However, in recent times, among mainstream therapy, there has been a greater willingness to recognise spirituality as an important part of what it means to be human (e.g. Assagioli 1991; Hay 2006; Heron 1998; Rowan 2005) and to develop approaches and interventions that include working with spiritual issues in counselling/ psychotherapy (Gubi 2008; Lines 2006; Moore and Purton 2006; Pargament 2007; Richards and Bergin 1997; West 2000, 2004). This has arguably led to a blurring of distinctions between spiritual direction/accompaniment and counselling/psychotherapy.

Working with the spiritual

Any definition of 'spirituality' that might be offered here could never adequately capture the 'felt sense' of the 'lived experience' from which meaning ultimately is gained on a personal level. To really understand spirituality, it is necessary to let go of our desire for absolute certainty, neat definitions and universally applicable categories in order to enter into an aspect of human experience that transcends final categorisation (Swinton 2001). Spirituality is ultimately about the search for meaning and fulfilment in life. It involves the desire to make sense and meaning out of life, to discover one's ultimate true nature and relationship to the universe (O'Murchu 1994). It involves a 'yearning within the human being for meaning for that which is greater than the encapsulated individual, for interconnection with all that is. It is an expression of the whole person, physical, emotional and intellectual' (Thorne 2001, p.438). The yearning includes a desire to become more in tune with one's authentic self in relation to others and to the world. It accommodates an openness to the infinite, to something beyond self to which one seeks connection and relationship that can give life meaning and purpose. Various spiritual traditions have created systems of relating to that which is 'transcendent' and 'ultimate'. For many, this sense of 'Ultimate Mystery' or 'Transcendent Other' can be related to and understood as God, Higher Self, Inner Light or Cosmos.

Pargament (2007) simply but profoundly defines spirituality as 'the search for the sacred'.

Swinton (2001) suggests that the central features of spirituality involve the search for the ontological significance of life in order to make sense of life situations and derive purpose in our existence. This leads to the creation of a value system from which beliefs and standards emerge that are to do with truth, beauty, worth of thought and behaviours, and which are often discussed as 'ultimate values'. Spirituality includes a sense of transcendence – the experience and appreciation of a dimension beyond self which can lead to expanding self-boundaries. Connecting with one's inner self, with others, with 'the ultimate' (e.g. God, Higher Power) and with the worthiness of the environment is also a central feature, as is a sense of 'becoming' – the unfolding of life, and the sense of life as a journey that demands an openness to experiencing and reflection from which one can gain a sense of 'who one is' and 'how one knows'. Spirituality contains an aspiration towards existential meaning that comes from a sense of the transpersonal but which is self-directed and inwardly focused. It possesses some sense of coherent universal meaning. It involves the interpersonal and the superpersonal. By interpersonal, I mean how I relate to 'the other' in the form of co-operative interactions and finding meaning from participation in a larger project. By superpersonal, I refer to relationships that are 'other directed' and outwardly focused – a sense of feeling of 'worth' because something is expected of me by life, God or something ultimate. Spirituality includes the use of various resources (e.g. ritual, chanting, breathing, mindfulness, imagery, prayer, meditation) and can be experienced as unsought exceptional human experience such as out-of-body experiences, dreams, past-life memories, telepathy, trance, apparitions, other-life experiences, healing, radiance, a sense of specialness, a sense of meaning and a sense of transcendence. It is this dimension to experiencing and faith that is the focus of spiritual accompaniment, and which is explored in counselling when a client's spirituality is worked with.

Spiritual accompaniment/direction

Spiritual accompaniment can be described as 'a ministry of presence and attentiveness' (Guenther 1993). Traditionally, it has been characterised by external notions of 'guidance', 'instruction' and 'formation' which was the role of monastic communities and specified 'spiritual fathers' (or mentors) who would teach and admonish (Merton 1960). However, Benner (2002) argues that giving advice, authoritarianism, disciplining, preaching, moral guidance, teaching and counselling are not part of spiritual accompaniment any more. More recently, spiritual accompaniment has become associated with insights gained from being in a state of 'deep spiritual hunger' (yearning) within the accompanee, that enables him/her to be open to hearing 'truths' at a deep spiritual level. Merton (1960) states that the function of the spiritual director is to encourage what is truly spiritual in the soul. He suggests that the spiritual director teaches the other to discern and distinguish what is truly good spiritually. S/he helps another 'to recognize and to follow the inspirations of grace in his/her life, in order to arrive at that to which God is leading' (p.17). At its most profound, spiritual accompaniment can best be thought of as an act of deep relational 'meeting' and 'hearing' where there is a sacredness of presence and collaboration of exploration conducted in a spirit of deep love and an awareness of the sacred. It involves attending to the soul of one's self and to the soul of the other. It constitutes the accompanier metaphorically and empathically 'walking alongside' the accompanee in her 'inner life journey' of yearning and/or celebration as a soul friend (Gubi 2015a). Spiritual accompaniment is the art of appropriately being alongside another in their spiritual journeying or quest. It is a way of insightfully hearing the process of spiritual journeying, a 'way of being' for meeting another on a spiritual level, and a 'way of being' for facilitating their journeying – however idiosyncratic and existential that journey may be (Gubi 2015b). Much of the literature on spiritual direction (e.g. Leech 1994; Mabry 2006; Moon and Benner 2004) now stresses the non-directive role of the spiritual director, and the importance of a mutually collaborative relationship. However, some people (e.g. Harborne 2015, p.125) still hold on to the nomenclature of 'spiritual direction' because it links current practice to its historical roots, and because it indicates a sense of journeying in a direction that is led by the Holy Spirit. In this book, the two nomenclatures of spiritual accompaniment and spiritual direction will be used interchangeably, as the issues that are explored in this book relate to both, if indeed they are different these days.

Spirituality in mainstream counselling/psychotherapy

As I have previously stated (Gubi 2015b), mainstream approaches to counselling have traditionally been informed theoretically and philosophically by the psychodynamic/psychoanalytic, the humanistic (including person-centred and gestalt), and the cognitive behavioural therapy (CBT)/rational-emotive 'schools' of psychology. By 1992, Dryden was claiming that there were more than 400 therapies (Dryden 1992), although many of them still maintain a theoretical base in one or more of the three traditional schools. Some approaches (e.g. human givens and CBT) are more directive than others (e.g. person-centred). These days, there is a greater requirement for evidence-based practice, and there is more dialogue and integration between the various approaches than there used to be. McLeod summarises the generic 'strategies' of all counselling/psychotherapy approaches as:

- using the conversation, dialogue and expressive techniques to develop understanding and create meaning in relation to problematic events and experiences, and to help a person to tell his or her story

- working with the client to identify aspects of thinking and behaviour that the client wishes to change...

- identifying ways of finding meaning and possibility in areas of bodily, felt, emotional experience that the person has reported as troubling...

- reviewing and reflecting on the life narrative of the person, with the goal of achieving a greater degree of coherence and self-acceptance...

- reviewing the cultural resources that are available to a person, and finding ways in which the possibilities arising from these resources can be put to use.

(McLeod 2009, p.13)

In the mainstream approaches to counselling and psychotherapy, religion and spirituality have largely been treated with the suspicion of having a proselytising, fundamentalist or evangelical agenda (Gubi 2001) and ridiculed as providing a crooked cure, as being infantile and foreign to reality (Gubi 2002) – a prejudice that is rooted in Freud's (1961) thinking. However, spirituality is more readily acknowledged in the mainstream counselling/psychotherapy literature as a valid human experience, a way of making meaning of life and a cultural resource that can be utilised (e.g. Gubi 2008; Lines 2006; Purton and Moore 2006; Pargament 2007; Richards and Bergin 1997; Swinton 2001; West 2000, 2004). There is a greater readiness by some prominent counsellors/psychotherapists to embrace the spiritual and to think of the counselling process in spiritual terms – for example, counselling as a sacred space, grace (West 2004), forgiveness (Ransley and Spy 2004), prayer and ritual (Gubi 2008), solitude and silence (Bazzano 2009), mindfulness (Segal, Williams and Teasdale 2001) and discernment (Thorne 2006), among other spiritual concepts and resources. Psychological theory has begun to encompass the spiritual (e.g. Rowan 2005).

Are counselling/psychotherapy and spiritual accompaniment/direction the same?

Harborne (2012) has asked what she calls her 'heretical question': could spiritual direction be considered to be a 'modality' of counselling/psychotherapy? In furthering her argument, Harborne states that within counselling/psychotherapy, there are already many differing and distinctive areas of work (e.g. addiction work, bereavement work, working with children and young people), each requiring a different approach. In gently teasing this idea out in a workshop at the 'Continuing the Journey' conference which I attended in 2016, Harborne patiently listened to her critics and then set the group a simple exercise. It was to draw a sort of Venn diagram – and to place a list of words within the 'intersection', or at either end – of what we felt was common or distinctive to counselling/psychotherapy and spiritual accompaniment/direction. The exercise was very thought-provoking. Table I.1 shows where I placed the words when working with a client of faith, but you may place them differently. Wherever you place the words, I would confidently state that there will be more words in the intersection than at either end, highlighting that they have more in common than is different – which is Harborne's challenge.

Table I.1: The similarities and differences between counselling/psychotherapy and spiritual accompaniment/direction

Distinctive to only counselling/psychotherapy	Shared by both counselling/psychotherapy and spiritual accompaniment/direction		Distinctive to only spiritual accompaniment/direction
	Ethics	God	
	Empathy	Vocation	
	Holy Spirit	Confidentiality	
	Presence	Love	
	Family life	Faith	
	Boundaries	Meeting	
	Self-awareness	Church	
	Feelings	Congruence	
	Presenting past	Supervision	
	Charism	Unconditional positive regard	
	Listening	Training	
	Life experience	Appropriate self-disclosure	
	Keeping notes	Current joys	
	Current problems	Speaking	
	Dual relationships	Truth	
	Prayer	Work	
	Self-awareness	Insurance	
	Reflection	Making meaning	
	Relationship	Patterns of behaviour	
	Spirituality		

The position of this book

However, rather than promoting the idea that they are the same, this book advances the perspective that counselling/psychotherapy and spiritual direction/accompaniment have more in common than they have differences when working with the spiritual dimension of people of faith – and that both disciplines (if, indeed, they are different) have much to learn from each other. This has implications for ethical practice, training and supervision. The chapter authors concur with Gubi's 'Relationship of Counselling to Spiritual Accompaniment' model

(Gubi 2015a, 2015b, 2011a) that counselling and spiritual accompaniment, when working with people of faith, involve an oscillation between soul-orientated issues and psychologically orientated issues, which require appropriate focus and responses. Each chapter author holds a Christian faith (each one being at a different place in faith on the broad spectrum that is Christianity – ranging from Pentecostal to liberal, to being agnostic but identifying more with Christianity than with any other spiritual tradition, to being contemplative). So, mostly they will use the language of Christianity, and of their therapeutic tradition and spiritual accompaniment tradition, to authentically explore the issues that are the focus for each chapter. However, it is hoped that the principles of what they are exploring can be translated across faith traditions so as to be inclusive of the reality that spiritual accompaniment/companionship is not a purely Christian endeavour.

The content and structure of this book

This book continues the work of *Spiritual Accompaniment and Counselling: Journeying with Psyche and Soul* (Gubi 2015a) in furthering the understanding of what it means to accompany, at depth, people who are exploring aspects of their spirituality in order to grow through the spiritual issues that trouble them, or to discern the spiritual path, or 'God's will', that enables them to move to a more authentic, or accepting, place within themselves.

In Chapter 1, Lynette Harborne considers what 'discernment' means in spiritual journeying, drawing on her experience of Ignatian spirituality. The chapter explores different strategies for enabling discernment and focuses on the centrality of prayer in that process. In Chapter 2, I (the Reverend Professor Peter Madsen Gubi) examine the use of prayer in counselling and spiritual accompaniment, and argue for the conscious consideration of ethical practice in what may seem a very natural spiritual resource that is at the heart of much spiritual encounter. In Chapter 3, Dr Phil Goss explores creative methods for exploring spirituality, using case examples from his experiences as a Jungian analyst. In Chapter 4, the Reverend Dr R. Jane Williams considers contemplative approaches to training spiritually literate counsellors (and, by implication, also spiritual accompaniers), drawing on her experience of training therapists in a theological seminary. In Chapter 5, I advocate the use of reflexive practice groups in supporting therapists and accompaniers, and in facilitating spiritual and theological development for counsellors, spiritual accompaniers, clergy and the wider church community. In Chapter 6, Ruth Bridges explores, in depth, the potential impact of existential crisis on spirituality, drawing on her own experience of personal loss, and of working with those who are dying. Dr Valda Swinton examines the impact of sexual abuse of spirituality in Chapter 7, and, in Chapter 8, Dr Nikki Kiyimba explores what it might mean to grow spiritually through traumatic events, and the impact on the counsellor or accompanier of working with such material. Finally, in Chapter 9, Professor William West elucidates some research that he undertook of counsellors and religious pastoral carers in dialogue. His research highlights the need for greater 'fluency' (i.e. the ability to move between the spiritual and the psychological) within therapists (and, by implication, within spiritual accompaniers), which has implications for training and supervision.

Who this book is for

This book is intended for therapists or folk who offer any kind of spiritual or pastoral accompaniment (both formally and informally) in whatever context. It is written to heighten their awareness in order to improve levels of competence in their encounters with others at a spiritual level, in the hope that that will be beneficial for the people we accompany. Throughout this book, it is assumed that counselling and psychotherapy are understood to be the same (although there is an appreciation that this is an ongoing debate (McLeod 2009)), and that the insights from them are also applicable to other helping contexts (e.g. chaplaincy, social work, ministry, nursing) in which people are encountered and accompanied in a one-to-one relationship. There is also an assumption that spiritual accompaniment and spiritual direction are the same, although some of the chapter contributors have their own preference for which term they use, depending on which tradition they are grounded in. Nevertheless, what is said about spiritual accompaniment is applicable to spiritual direction and vice versa.

Chapter 1

Exploring Discernment

Lynette Harborne

Introduction

In this chapter, I will consider what is meant by the term 'discernment', particularly, but not exclusively, in an Ignatian context. I will explore the practice of discernment and identify a range of different strategies; I will also reflect on the process of both individual and group discernment, drawing on my personal experience. Throughout the chapter, the centrality of prayer in the discernment process will be emphasised.

My personal context

My practice as a psychotherapist is in a secular context, but my practice as a spiritual director is overtly Christian, and I draw substantially on the Christian tradition and literature in this chapter. However, I do not define myself as a 'Christian counsellor', with all the possible preconceptions and implications that this may have for some people in relation to biblical understanding and doctrine. I see myself much more as a psychotherapist who happens to be a Christian. Some of my therapy clients are Christians, some are clergy, some are religious, but many are completely unaware of my personal faith background. If it seems appropriate, I am willing to address both general spiritual and specifically religious issues in my work as a psychotherapist, and also to address psychological issues in spiritual direction. However, as I have explored elsewhere (Harborne 2012), I always hold in mind that there may be contractual and content differences between therapy and spiritual direction.

I am, therefore, aware that this chapter may have more relevance for readers who are spiritual directors, pastoral care workers and therapists working within a Christian framework than perhaps for others engaged in psychotherapy and counselling, where drawing on a specifically Christian 'model' might be seen as inappropriate. However, I hope that all readers will find ideas, insights and, in particular, strategies that may be transferable and relevant across contexts.

I have already explained my personal approach to the vocabulary of spiritual direction and spiritual accompaniment (Harborne 2012, 2014, 2015), where I have expressed my belief that my role as a spiritual director is not about being directive and telling a directee what to think or do, but much more about accompanying someone in finding the direction of their own spiritual journey – a direction that is in line with the will of God. As I have also previously stated, I personally very much appreciate and value my association with the long history of what has traditionally been known as spiritual direction. The question of terminology and vocabulary has a particular relevance in a chapter on discernment, as I have recently heard discussions about whether it is exactly this issue that is the main difference between what is called spiritual direction and what is called spiritual accompaniment. This may be a false dichotomy, but it raises an interesting question which, for therapists, may seem to have resonances with the continuing discussions about the differences between counselling and psychotherapy, although in the latter case the differentiating criteria are much more clearly defined.

What do we mean by 'discernment'?

Giallanza (1998, p.21) points out, 'Etymologically, discernment means "to separate apart", that is, to distinguish something so it can be perceived clearly.' The *Oxford Paperback Dictionary* (2009, p.260) defines discernment as 'showing good judgement', which is something that would probably be seen as desirable in any context. When considering discernment as part of the spiritual direction process, I assume that 'showing good judgement' will include paying attention to God, with a desire to discover what his plan for us might be. We may have evidence of God's will in the teaching, life and example of Jesus Christ, but we nevertheless often lack clarity about the way forward in a particular situation in our own life. As Giallanza also points out, we may benefit from the involvement of others who will offer wisdom and insight, and who may hold us accountable as part of our decision-making. Although recognising the dangers of a discernment process lapsing into procrastination, Giallanza suggests that it may take a period of time, both for considerable reflection and also in order to gather relevant information on the basis of which to make a decision (1998, p.24).

At the core of discernment is the desire to discover and to follow God's will. As Merton (1953, p.27) states, 'The presence of discernment and detachment is manifested by a spontaneous thirst for what is good – charity, union with the will of God…' Sweeney (1988, p.354) points out:

> Most treatises on Christian discernment identify Jesus' teaching: 'By their fruits you shall know them' (Matthew 7:16) as the general principle of discernment in the gospels. In other words, the ultimate test of an authentic movement of the Holy Spirit…is its enduring fruitfulness… Specifically, this implies that the test of the authenticity of any approach to discernment or spiritual direction is its effectiveness in guiding a person to union with the Father and loving service of humankind. Above all, discernment is a matter of faith, and, as Hebrews 11:1 tells us, 'Faith is the substance of things hoped for, the evidence of things not seen.'

Dougherty (1995, p.25), when reflecting on discernment in the Christian tradition, locates it firmly in prayer, stating, 'Prayer, then, is the starting place for discernment… It fine-tunes the heart to the prayer of God in us, God's desire for us.' She goes on to discuss how prayer changes and, in itself, requires discernment, asking ourselves whether our prayer continues 'to honour and reflect God's presence in my life?' She comments, 'Discernment on prayer is really prayer about our prayer. In this prayer we open ourselves to God's gaze, looking with God at God's desire for us, our desire for God, noticing how our prayer reflects these desires' (p.27).

Instead of asking the question 'Am I making the right decision?', it might be better to pay attention to the question 'Am I trusting God enough and being led by love?' Dougherty (1995, p.33) puts it very succinctly: '[T]here comes a time when we are invited into simple faith as we make decisions, trusting God to transform the ambiguity of our hearts with the fire of love and to be with us in and through the uncertainty.' Similarly, Runcorn (2003, p.5) expresses the view that:

> [G]uidance is not a technique to be mastered but life to be entered. The question, 'What decision is God guiding me to make?' is part of a much bigger and more important question: 'What kind of person is God willing that I may become?'

The assertion that prayer is central to the process of discernment obviously raises the question 'What is prayer?', which in turn leads to the (very Ignatian) idea of finding God in all things, moving us away from the idea of 'praying for…' towards that of engaging fully with God's presence in the world. Muldoon (2004, p.185), writing about the nature of prayer he experiences when walking, cycling or rowing, states, 'In time, we must all learn that it is not we who are praying but God who is praying because we allow it to happen. The most authentic prayer, then, will not happen when we schedule it.' Through prayer, we can discover – uncover perhaps – what God wills for us and what is our true vocation. As Newman (1925, p.5) writes, 'God has created me to do Him some definite service; He has committed some work to me which He has not committed to another. I have my mission…'

However, discernment as a process is by no means exclusively a Christian activity. Dougherty (1995) helpfully gives examples from the Sioux Indian tradition of enlightenment through 'The Eye of the Great Spirit'; from the Hindu literature of 'Braham is all… To know him…is to untie the knot of ignorance'; and from Buddhism wisdom: 'When you look into your true self, whatever is deeper is found right there.' Dougherty also points out that, in the yogic traditions, 'the word for discernment is "viveka" which means "to sense the will of God in the moment"' (pp.24–25).

Discernment and St Ignatius of Loyola

In the Christian tradition, the process of discernment is perhaps particularly associated with the life and writings of St Ignatius of Loyola, founder of the Society of Jesus – the Jesuits. As a soldier in Spain, his goal was to become a great knight, but being hit by a cannon ball in the battle of Pamplona in 1521 put paid to that ambition. It was during his convalescence in the castle of Loyola that he was drawn to imitate the life of the saints, and to love and serve God. His vocation led him to the foundation of the Jesuits, and to writing his *Spiritual Exercises* (Fleming 1996).

Toner (1982) summarises the core of Ignatius' *Spiritual Exercises* as follows: 'The overall goal is the removal of obstacles in us to the one certain expression of love for God, our seeking sincerely to find and do his will' (p.341). At the heart of the discernment process is the necessity to surrender our will to that of God in order to experience true spiritual freedom (Fleming 1996, p.23).

Ignatian spirituality

Ignatian concepts are based on the following assumptions (Fleming 1996, pp.136–137 and pp.243–249):

- Discernment is always between options which are good in themselves.

- I am seeking to do God's will.

- God never wills me to choose evil or infidelity to my vocational commitments.

- It is characteristic of God to give genuine happiness and spiritual joy.

- It is characteristic of the destructive spirit to fight against this happiness.

However, in practice this does not mean that the consequence of a true discernment process will necessarily and immediately bring a sense of happiness and joy; God's timing may be very different from ours.

Ignatius and the discernment of spirits

However, discernment is about much more than making decisions and choices. It is also about being able to differentiate between what does and does not come from God. In Ignatian terms, this is identified by a sense of 'consolation', or bringing us closer to God, and what leaves us with a sense of 'desolation', or being further away from God (Fleming 1996, pp.247–269). Ignatius, reflecting the culture of the 16th century, uses the language of 'the evil one' and 'the false lights of Lucifer' when writing about discernment between good and ill, which some readers may not find helpful language. However, the ideas that he explores around being willing to follow the example of Christ in terms of poverty, self-giving and humility, rather than being drawn to wealth, ego and pride, are perfectly transferable and relevant to 21st-century language.

Toner (1982) also points out that Ignatius addresses the question of discernment very much in terms of the internal spiritual journey rather than the external (p.39). The phrase *discernment of spirits* indicates openness to, and awareness of, the difference between what is coming from God and what is coming from 'the evil one'. Toner goes on to state that 'Ignatius' rules are concerned with inner, private events, the moments in the individual discerner's own mind and heart prior to even his own overt acts which flow from these inner movements' (p.342), suggesting the necessity for a deep level of self-awareness which would also be recognised in the therapeutic process. Ignatius suggests that, in seeking to follow God, individuals may well experience temptations from 'the evil spirit' and, if they truly desire to align their will with that of God, their response will be affected by conscience or by feelings of encouragement, joy and peace.

Ignatius also suggests that, when seeking discernment, it is desirable that we start from a position of indifference, having no preference for one outcome or the other. He offers us the image of a 'balance at equilibrium' (Fleming 1996, p.141), indicating no differentiating weight between the two sides. In this state, we are more likely to be open to the promptings of the Holy Spirit, and therefore to responding to the will of God. As Dailey (1997) points out, this was also reflected in the views and writing of Francis de Sales (1995), who, having been much influenced by his Jesuit education, wrote, 'Provided the name of God is sanctified...that His will is done, then the soul cares for nothing else' (Dailey 1997, p.234).

Ignatius identifies two kinds of life choices: the first relating to major life decisions such as whether to marry, to have children, to take a particular career path; and the second relating to changes we might make to the life we are currently leading – for example, change jobs, move house, embark on further training. In making such decisions, Ignatius emphasises that:

> [M]y whole aim should be to seek to respond to this God so actively working with me in giving direction to my life. Keeping clearly before me my desire to serve and praise God our Lord, I can begin to search out the means...for all these choices are means helping me to live my

life in God's service and so to deepen my love relationship with God.
(Fleming 1996, p.135)

Ignatius is also quite clear about how to act when experiencing a
period of desolation: 'When we find ourselves weighed down by
a certain desolation, we should not try to change a previous decision
or come to a new decision' (Fleming 1996, p.251).

The practice of discernment

However, I would not want to give the impression that engaging in a
process of discernment is exclusive to Ignatian practice, as it is common
in many other denominations and faith communities. For example,
when members of the Society of Friends, the Quakers, engage in a
'Meeting for Business', they are undertaking a discernment process.
At such a meeting, the matter to be addressed will be clearly known
by all those present. The meeting will begin, and end, with time for
reflection in the Quaker tradition, during which time the business to
be addressed will be held in mind. The process is very much one
of listening and reflecting, rather than discussing. Participants are
encouraged to allow silence before and after each person speaks, and
to describe their own experience as genuinely as possible. It is not an
opportunity to critique or discuss what someone else has said, but to
listen with full attention and to allow each person's contribution
to be respectfully heard. Through this discernment process, the matter
under consideration can be addressed and a conclusion reached. There
is no voting, no imposition of a majority view; rather, it is a process of
reaching a decision by mutual understanding and consensus. This is an
example of group discernment in practice.

In the Methodist tradition, what is known as the 'Quadrilateral'
draws on scripture, tradition, reason and experience, which are
all aspects that need to be taken into account in any discernment
process. In the Benedictine tradition, Neuman (1988, p.43) suggests
that '[a] revisionist method of theology, such as the one outlined by
David Tracy, should be introduced more forcefully into the realm of
spirituality'. Tracy's (1975) model invites dialogue between theology
and contemporary disciplines, as well as scripture and tradition, and
suggests that theology should no longer hold a privileged position
and should acknowledge the possibility of mutual transformation from

such a dialogue (p.49). This view is supported by Lyall (2001, p.34) who writes of 'a process of mutual giving and receiving'. This understanding of scripture and tradition is echoed by retired Anglican bishop Richard Holloway (1999, p.80), who states that 'we should not shirk the task of rethinking the authority of the Bible over our lives, allowing the living scripture of our own experience to challenge the dead letter of the written law'. It can be argued that the above revisionist models all resonate with the concept of 'finding God in all things'.

As we can therefore see, the Quaker, Methodist (Wesley), Roman Catholic (Tracy) and Anglican (Holloway) traditions all advocate engaging a variety of factors, including reason, human experience, scripture and tradition, in the process of reflection that contributes to the discernment process.

The process of discernment

Unfortunately – or perhaps fortunately – God does not skywrite His intentions or instructions, and, in reflecting on the question of discernment, it is always helpful to remember that it is a process rather than an event. Discernment is a matter of faith, and even when we have undertaken a discernment process with clear commitment and firm intention, there may not be absolute clarity, and we may still have to act in faith despite doubts and uncertainty. So discernment is much more than just making a choice or decision.

Gallagher (2009, p.7), a Jesuit, suggests three stages in the discernment process: *preparation, discernment* and *fruit.*

Preparation

In order to be a person who is prepared to choose God's will, the Ignatian tradition suggests that we first need to recognise the foundational awareness of God's infinite love for us and that 'Man [*sic*] is created to praise, reverence and service God our Lord' (Puhl 1997, p.20). The further suggestion is that we may predispose ourselves to seek God's will by engaging in spiritual exercises – for example, retreats, spiritual direction, the daily Examen (Muldoon 2004), the process of reviewing the events of the day, the Eucharist, the contemplation of Christ in the Gospels, and periods of silence.

Discernment

Ignatius describes how this may come through a moment of clarity, but recognises that this is not always so. He states: 'There is a time of clarity which comes with undeviating persistence. We think of the dramatic change in St Paul on the road to Damascus' (Fleming 1996, p.139). However, discernment may also come with considerably less clarity: 'Quite frequently we experience a time of alternating certainties and doubts...of consolation and of desolation' (p.139). Ignatius also acknowledges that there may be complete uncertainty in discernment: 'Sometimes, through no fault of our own, nothings seems to be going on... The free and peaceful use of our reasoning abilities shows forth the calm logic of this time' (p.139).

Fruits

Ignatius does not suggest that the discernment process will necessarily be completed without effort and persistence on our part (Fleming 1996, p.249). This process is an exercise in trust, and will, in itself, be richly blessed by God's grace as described in 1 Corinthians 15.10: 'I worked harder than any of them – though it was not I, but the grace of God that is with me.' It is not just a matter of identifying 'a result'; the process is as grace-filled as the outcome, a view that was recently expressed in private correspondence from a Roman Catholic seminarian:

> I guess some people have great clarity, whereas the rest of us just muddle on, asking questions and never being sure about answers! Perhaps asking the question and trying to work out the answer *is* our vocation and all that God really desires of us...

Discernment and spiritual direction

Discernment, therefore, can be considered to be primarily a matter of prayer and relationship with God. However, in order to engage wholeheartedly in the process, we may find that the opportunity to discuss the process of discernment with another is helpful, and discernment is often central to the content of spiritual direction. Spiritual direction provides us with a space in which to explore issues of discernment with someone who is willing to walk alongside us in our spiritual journey.

However, despite the undoubted benefits that spiritual direction may offer, it must nevertheless be acknowledged that it is not for everyone, and does not even sit well in all Christian traditions. Despite telephone and the advent of email, Skype, Facetime and other means of electronic communication, in some situations or circumstances it is just not practical or possible. It would also be far too sweeping a statement to suggest that spiritual direction would be beneficial for absolutely everyone. Although it may provide a valuable resource for some, clearly the process of prayerful reflection on decisions and choices is not exclusive to spiritual direction.

Strategies for discernment

Ignatius suggests a number of strategies for making a good choice and, as we have already seen, his initial instruction to 'try to be like a balance at equilibrium, without leaning to either side' (Fleming 1996, p.141) emphasises the importance of starting with a sense of openness and disinterest (in the true sense of the word) in the actual outcome. Some Ignatian suggestions are included below, together with some from other sources. It is important to recognise the value of paying attention to the feelings that arise and emerge through engaging in these exercises. Although making rational decisions clearly demands logical thinking, there is more to the process than that, and it is also important to notice our 'gut feelings' and to draw on all our senses. We are more than just thinking beings; we acquire and process information in many other ways, and this is reflected throughout the Ignatian exercises. Above all lies the question of whether our decision will help us to live with greater faith, hope and love, and be instrumental in developing our relationship with God. Will it help us to live out our own personal vocation?

Four columns

The four-column exercise identifies advantages and disadvantages of any situation and choice. For example, if the decision is about changing jobs, the four columns would be headed as follows:

The advantages of changing jobs

The disadvantages of changing jobs

The advantages of not changing jobs

The disadvantages of not changing jobs.

Having undertaken the exercise, confirmation is sought through prayer (Fleming 1996, p.143). This activity offers what amounts to an in-depth cost/benefit exercise which, in turn, has similarities with a SWOT analysis – a process that is often used in a commercial context, in which Strengths, Weaknesses, Opportunities and Threats in any situation are identified and noted.

Advice to another

You are invited to imagine that you are giving advice to someone whom you do not know, but for whom you want the best, and then to pay attention to what that advice might be.

End-of-life reflection

This exercise invites you to imagine how, on your deathbed, you might view a decision made during your life to reflect on what decision you might wish you had made.

Advice from an older to a younger 'self'

Alternatively, you might reflect on how, at a much later stage in life, you might consider what your older self might now say to your younger self. Or you might imagine yourself having a conversation with someone else – someone older and wiser than you – and to imagine what they might possibly be saying.

Conversation with God

In this exercise you consider having a conversation with God about a decision after your death and what feelings this would evoke.

Personal obituary

When making a major decision, you might also find it useful to imagine your own obituary – or even write it – and reflect on the decision made and the impact that this has on you as you reflect.

Live as...

When a decision can clearly be divided into two possible ways forward, either this or that, yes or no, now or later, then it can be helpful and revealing to live as wholeheartedly as possible for a specified length of time, as though the decision has been made one way, and then repeat the exercise with the alternative decision. The length of time will vary depending on circumstances, but it might be as long as nine months (a full gestation period), or a year, a month, a week, a day, an hour. Valuable insights can emerge by paying attention to the nuances of the responses we experience throughout this process.

Creative imagination exercise

In this exercise, you carefully read a Gospel passage several times and then settle down to imagine yourself as one of the participants, observers or bystanders in the scene described. Imagine where you are in relation to Jesus. Are you near him or some distance away? What are you wearing? What can you see, hear, touch, taste? Engage all your senses in order to feel part of the scene. What might Jesus say to you? What are your feelings? This exercise may give you a clearer sense of God's will in any particular situation.

Compass and four seasons exercise

In a similar way, Thompson, Pattison and Thompson (2008, p.214), drawing on Runcorn's work (2003), suggest a model based on linking different aspects of any situation with the points of the compass and the seasons as follows:

North	Fixed points/values (non-negotiable)	Winter
South	Recreation and enjoyment	Summer
East	What is new and surprising	Spring
West	What is in decline (time to let go)	Autumn

This can be a particularly helpful process in a group situation, where individuals hold very differing views about change. Somehow, it seems less personally threatening to acknowledge, both to self and others, what feels non-negotiable (winter) while accepting that for someone else this may feel in decline (autumn). Through this discernment process, any perceived threats may be diminished and the potential and climate for change can be developed.

Journalling

When struggling with an issue of discernment, the journalling process can be very helpful. You might write a description of the situation in which you find yourself, and identify the decision, or decisions, that need to be made. You may describe the dilemmas you are facing and the feelings with which you are wrestling. Keeping a journal can help to bring clarity to a situation, and rereading what you have previously written can also be enlightening and encouraging – 'Did I really feel like that not so long ago? How things have changed since I made that entry! Looking back, I can more clearly where God has been working in my life since I started to face this question or dilemma.' As Merton (1953, p.201) writes:

> Keeping a journal has taught me that there is not so much new in your life as you sometimes think. When you reread your journal, you find out that your latest discovery is something you already found out about five years ago. Still it is true that one penetrates deeper and deeper into the same ideas and the same experience.

There is no one particular way to keep a journal, but personally I have found *How to Keep a Spiritual Journal* by Klug (2002) gives some helpful and creative ideas.

Letter to/from God

As part of keeping a spiritual journal, you may find that writing a letter to God and/or a letter from God is a helpful activity. Being completely honest and open about your feelings can be very revealing; highlighting what is really going on for you, not just on the surface but at a greater depth, is a process that can have quite surprising results. Giving yourself permission to express feelings of anger or disappointment in this way can feel liberating.

Lectio Divina

Using the Bible as a basis for prayer and discernment can clearly be a source of inspiration. However, the dangers of 'proof-texting' to support a decision already made cannot be ignored. As Oliver (2006, pp.43–44) states:

> Treating the Bible as some kind of literary Pope that utters holy truth without regard for circumstance or context will only serve to close some issues that should be left open to the speaking of God. Simple proof-texting…undermines the whole idea of the Bible as revealing the word of God.

Lectio Divina, however, can be very different. It has four parts – *lectio, meditatio, oratio* and *contemplatio* – and engaging in this form of Bible study can shed light on questions of discernment.

> *Lectio:* A passage of scripture is read slowly and more than once, the reader being alert to any particular word, phrase, idea or image that has a particular impact.

> *Meditatio:* The reader savours what has had particular significance, pondering on what the personal message of this might be, what it might be saying, where it might be leading.

> *Oratio: Meditatio* is followed by a period of prayer (*oratio*), in which you offer yourself to God with the desire of aligning your will with His.

> *Contemplatio:* Prayer ends with a period of resting in God's love.

Theological reflection as discernment

The process of theological reflection offers a helpful and developmental model of discernment, an example of which is described in Thompson, Pattison and Thompson (2008). The first step is to write down a description and definition of the situation being explored, and subsequently flesh it out with the thoughts, feelings and images that come to mind, perhaps in a spidergram or other diagrammatic format.

The next step is to consider links between what has emerged in this initial activity and any scriptural passages, prayers, other spiritual writings or events with which you are familiar, and then to spend time contemplating these in a prayerful way.

My experience has been that undertaking this exercise as an unhurried activity can help to identify and uncover insights and feelings that were not originally recognised, and which may add considerable significance and weight to the discernment process.

The discernment experience

The above may all be creative strategies that are helpful in the discernment process. However, as already stated, discernment is often not merely about a choice for one action rather than another. Discernment may well involve a long process, with what may appear to be 'mistakes' along the way. In considering the whole process of discernment, I am reminded of the feelings that have emerged from my experience of a labyrinth, an experience that can be either physical, as when walking a labyrinth such as the one in Chartres Cathedral, or more metaphorical, by tracing an image on paper with your finger. In both cases, just when I seem to be 'getting somewhere' and heading for the centre, I find myself apparently travelling in the wrong direction towards the perimeter. With this in mind, it is worth reflecting on the difference between a labyrinth and a maze. A maze includes many dead ends and reversals; in fact, these are all part of the fun. In a labyrinth, however, the path will ultimately lead you to the still point at the centre, even if the journey at times seems somewhat circuitous.

However, these distinctions are not always clear when actually seeking to discern a way forward, as I know only too well from my own experience. Some years ago I found myself in a situation where a major life choice was necessary – a choice that involved discerning God's will and my personal vocation. I very much wanted to be faithful to God's will in my discernment of the way forward and spent a great deal of time in prayer and reflection. I went on retreat, I journalled, I sought advice from more experienced and wiser colleagues, friends and family. All this took well over a year, during which time I received much external affirmation to go ahead in a particular way, as well as a strong inner sense of confirmation. As a result of this strong sense, I made the decision to be proactive in attempting to take this particular project forward. I then ran into a brick wall which, at first, seemed to be a denial and negation of all the affirmation that I had previously received.

What did this teach me about discernment? It could have seemed that the whole process had been a complete waste of time – that I had deluded myself, and others, and that the process could not be trusted. But this was not my experience. True, I had experienced great disappointment at the outcome, but it was the very fact of the door being slammed firmly shut right in my face, and the sense of confusion and shame that I experienced as a result, that led me into personal psychotherapy and spiritual direction for the first time. This, in turn, led me to train and to develop a practice in both disciplines – a practice that has now been central to my life for a quarter of a century, and which I believe to be my true vocation.

So, although, in my case, the discernment process appeared at one point to have been, at best, mistaken and, at worst, pointless, in fact looking back I can now see quite clearly God's purpose throughout. The Christian story is full of instances of individuals seeking either to discover or to follow God's will for their life – their vocation – in very diverse situations, and often with unexpected consequences. Think of Abraham and Isaac (Genesis 22.1–19), of Moses (Exodus 12), of Samuel (1 Samuel 3), of Elijah (1 Kings 18), of Mary (Luke 1.26–38), of Peter (Acts 1), of Paul (Acts 9). Think perhaps of your own experience when you may have been convinced that you should follow one course of action, only later to discover that God's plan for you was very different indeed. Muldoon, calling to mind Hughes' (1985) book *God of Surprises*, reminds us that God is 'a person whose presence in our lives often calls us beyond the narrow limits of our expectations' (Muldoon 2004, p. 3). This is perhaps one of the most important aspects of trying to discern our vocation, and one of which I was aware almost daily in my work with Roman Catholic seminarians over a period of nearly ten years. We are called to be faithful in responding to God's invitation as we understand it, but it is the faithfulness of our response that is significant, not necessarily the outcome, which we may very mistakenly see as the goal. In the case of the seminarians with whom I worked, the commitment to the life-changing experience of six or more years of formation and the learning that this engendered may in themselves have been the true purpose. Ordination may, or may not, be part of their vocation, but in the process nothing is wasted. As Tetlow says

(2008, p.107), 'When we decide that we have discerned what God wants done and choose to do it, we have not reached certainty. We have reached hope-filled enactment.'

It is perhaps also encouraging for us in such circumstances to reflect on the experience of Ignatius himself. All his plans to be a successful soldier came to nothing, and he faced disappointment and failure after the battle of Pamplona. However, it was at this moment of apparent failure that his true vocation emerged – and I love the idea that the foundation of the Society of Jesus, the Jesuits, was in fact Plan B for Ignatius!

When discernment is unexpected

Sometimes discernment, or confirmation of discernment, can come to us with great clarity and in an entirely unexpected way from an unexpected external source. I remember an occasion in my own life when I was wrestling with uncertainty about the way forward in a particular situation, and I went on retreat with this very much on my mind. After the final Eucharist, and as I was preparing to leave the retreat centre, another retreatant, with whom I had had no contact or conversation whatsoever during the previous four days, came up to me and, somewhat hesitantly, said that she felt that God was telling her to pass on to me some very specific words. These words did not make much sense to her, but they spoke with complete clarity into my personal circumstances, giving me great – and completely unexpected – encouragement and consolation.

Discernment and psychotherapy

When engaging in serious and potentially life-changing discernment, it may make very sound sense to check out our thoughts, feelings and decisions with someone whose wisdom we value and appreciate – whether a family member, a friend, a work colleague or a spiritual director. Sometimes it can also be helpful to engage in psychotherapy or counselling, which can provide an environment in which to explore particular issues of discernment, by examining personal motives, options, patterns of behaviour, possible outcomes and likely consequences, as well as considering the possibility of unconscious processes that may be having unrecognised influence. If a therapist is working holistically, then it should be possible for spiritual aspects, and even specifically religious ones, to be included in the process.

Group discernment

A few years ago I was a member of a group that met regularly once a month to engage in a discernment process, focusing on a particular issue or dilemma. Because of the context of the group, the subject chosen for discernment often, but not invariably, related to church matters, but there was always an initial discussion about what the focus would be and sometimes more than one topic would be agreed. A passage of scripture would then be read twice to the group, with a pause between the two readings for reflection, and then there would be a period of silence and meditation for approximately half an hour, after which time each member of the group would contribute anything that had arisen for them in the silence in terms of reflections, words or images. As in the case of the Quaker practice, there would be a period of silence between each contribution and there would be no comment or discussion, just attentive and respectful listening.

I found this reflective process enlightening, and on some occasions even inspirational. The fact of being with other people who were all holding the same intention in prayer for a sustained amount of time, rather than the rather brief 'shopping list' approach that often seems to form part of church services, felt very powerful – an experience that gave a real sense of 'two or three being gathered together' in the presence of God.

Conclusion

To summarise, discernment is not an event; it is a process throughout which we must prayerfully hold in mind our desire to do God's will, and in which we seek to deepen our relationship with God and to explore our true vocation.

Chapter 2

Using Prayer in Counselling and Spiritual Accompaniment

Peter Madsen Gubi

Introduction

Many would probably argue that the use of prayer is one of the significant differences between counselling and spiritual accompaniment, with prayer seeming to have a more natural home within spiritual accompaniment, because accompaniers, and those whom they accompany, meet in encounter to explore and discern spiritual issues – and prayer is at the centre of all spirituality. However, I will argue in this chapter, as I have argued elsewhere (e.g. Gubi 2008, 2011b, 2009a), that prayer also has a natural place in counselling when working with people of faith, and although prayer may seem to belong more in spiritual accompaniment (simply because it is a more obvious place to explore spiritual matters), the ethical considerations of its integration are just as applicable in spiritual accompaniment as they are in counselling and psychotherapy. Its use in a natural setting does not preclude ethics!

I have personally never prayed *with* a client in my role as a counsellor, even when working with people of faith – but I certainly have prayed *for* clients and accompanees, and I have always asked their permission to do so. I have never presumed it was OK. I have sometimes (although not always) prayed with others in my role as priest and spiritual accompanier – again, always asking their permission, but also trying to discern if they could say 'No' if they wanted to (which is mostly met with a quizzical look of 'Of course it is OK! What a strange question to ask…'). I have had others pray with me, and have sometimes found it to be a cathartic and healing experience. However, I have also had others pray with me without asking, on the presumption that it would be acceptable to me as a Christian priest. The thought to ask if it would be OK never crossed their mind, because praying is firmly embedded in much Christian acculturation and culture, in that Christians often always begin and end meetings with a prayer. Although I went along with it and did not challenge it at the time, sometimes it has felt uncomfortable and inappropriate – especially when the prayer becomes about what the person praying wants to happen, rather than praying for God's will to be done in a situation. So, even in spiritual accompaniment, we cannot presume that it is OK to pray. This chapter, then, will look at the implications for practice of the use of prayer, drawing heavily on recommendations that I have made as a result of my research and practice in this area (Gubi 2008).

Prayer in practice

There is certainly evidence in the literature that prayer influences some counselling (Gubi 2008; Rose 2002; VanZant 2010; Wimberley 1990), with 59 per cent of BACP[1] accredited counsellors using prayer to support their work with clients and 12 per cent of BACP accredited counsellors having prayed with clients (Gubi 2002, 2004). So prayer cannot be identified as a difference between counselling and spiritual accompaniment, even if it is more likely to be encountered in the latter. It is important that there is an informed debate about the value of prayer as a spiritual intervention in both counselling and spiritual accompaniment, and that the limitation and value of such practice is critically evaluated to determine what it means in practice to work with a client's spirituality (Foskett and Lynch 2001). So, what might 'considerations for good practice' look like in the integration of prayer in counselling and spiritual accompaniment?

At a *philosophical level*, all counselling and spiritual accompaniment can be regarded as prayer. Prayer pervades the atmosphere and environment in which the counsellor and client, and accompanier and accompanee, are in 'communion' (encounter) at a spiritual level. Prayer is an attitude that is inherent in the counsellor's and accompanier's

---

1   British Association for Counselling and Psychotherapy.

way of being, providing a context for silence, defining the quality of attention and qualifying the sense of being a part of something bigger to which the work can be entrusted. Prayer provides an existential perspective, or frame of reference, that makes the work more meaningful at a spiritual level. This is motivational for the counsellor and accompanier, and provides a way of understanding the process of their work. Counselling and spiritual accompaniment are both 'prayer in action' (Canda 1990).

At a *covert level*, prayer is a valuable, integral and necessary part of the counsellor's and accompanier's supportive practice. It is a personal and private practice in which the counsellor, or accompanier, uses prayer: to ground and attune herself in preparation for the work, enabling a deeper level of presence, stillness, balance and concentration; to place the work in the care of a higher being, enabling connection with the 'here and now' and containment; to add an extra healing dimension to the work through the use of intercessory prayer on behalf of the client (or accompanee), which also enables the spiritual aspect of the work to be kept in focus; to still the mind, aiding peace, calm, meaning, purpose and direction at times of stuckness, panic and anxiety. This helps the counsellor or accompanier to stay with the 'not knowing' and the 'aloneness', enabling the connection with the client or accompanee to be maintained and enhanced; to stay with the intense feelings of helplessness, hopelessness and despair, as part of a spiritual discipline that enables the counsellor, or accompanier, to acknowledge her own spirituality, prevent burnout and maintain balance in her life through fostering a forum in which self-reflection, self-respect and self-care are intrinsic.

The counsellor or accompanier may also be upheld by the client's or accompanee's prayer at this level, providing that such practice is not explicitly encouraged, but instead accepted in the 'spirit' in which it is offered, even though at an unconscious level it may indicate issues of attachment and insecurity. The ethical use of prayer at the covert level is determined by the intent of the counsellor or accompanier, in that praying for the client or accompanee utilises a spiritual resource on behalf their client or accompanee. This can strengthen the relationship between counsellor and client, and accompanier and accompanee, because it taps into the forces that become 'powerfully operative in the transcendent encounter' (Thorne 1994, 1998, 2002). If the client or accompanee knows that the counsellor or accompanier does this, it can add to their sense of being cared for, and can reduce the sense of abandonment and separation that they may feel between sessions. However, it is important to avoid an unhealthy preoccupation with a client or accompanee in the counsellor's or accompanier's prayer life (Thorne 1998, pp.98–99). Magaletta and Brawer (1998) indicate that it is preferable to gain their consent, but it may be unethical to withhold such a practice if the counsellor or accompanier believes in the effectiveness of praying for clients or accompanees away from their presence (Gubi 2001). This has to be balanced against the perceived reaction of the client or accompanee if she knew that intercessory prayer was being enacted on her behalf without her permission. When the counsellor or accompanier prays on the client's or accompanee's behalf, it is ethically less problematic to use the 'Thy will be done' approach (Magaletta and Brawer 1998). This approach to prayer gives the work a more meaningful perspective by reminding the counsellor and accompanier that the process is part of something bigger than what takes place in the room, and is largely undetermined, full of 'unknowing' and out of the counsellor's or accompanier's control. The practice also serves to remind the counsellor and accompanier that her accountability is also to something greater, as well as to the client or accompanee. This can prevent complacency.

At the *overt level*, prayer can be used tentatively with a client or accompanee who is open to the process of prayer. However, the use of prayer needs to be carefully considered. My research (Gubi 2008) shows that praying overtly is most likely to occur at the beginning of a session, at the end of a session, at the termination of a counselling or accompaniment relationship, at times of desperation, through the use of silence, through the use of ritual, through transpersonal imaging (i.e. imagine what God or Higher Wisdom might say or do in this situation) and as a way of communicating appropriate values to the client that are compatible with intrinsic counselling or accompaniment values (e.g. 'We pray for Sam who we know is of great worth to you, and who is loved intensely by you, even though he can't yet see or know it for himself').

Considerations for good practice

Each of these three levels (i.e. philosophical, covert and overt) has to be *equally underpinned* by an ethical awareness based on the values of fidelity, autonomy, beneficence, non-maleficence, justice and self-respect which form the ethical framework for good practice (BACP 2016) in many ethical frameworks or codes. Considerations for good practice advocated here are underpinned by: (1) an awareness of potential ethical issues; (2) an awareness of how prayer can be integrated ethically; (3) an awareness of the quality and characteristics of the prayer being used; and (4) a considered awareness of issues of tension and difficulty for the counsellor.

Developing an awareness of potential ethical issues

The first consideration for good practice is the development of an awareness of potential ethical issues. It is clear from the literature (e.g. Magaletta and Brawer 1998) that the use of prayer is contentious and potentially fraught with difficulty (see Table 2.1).

An awareness of, and insight into, these difficulties is important in preventing the counsellor or accompanier from colluding with defences and resistance. However, the ethical difficulties, although cautionary, are not prohibitive if prayer is integrated appropriately into practice. A good counsellor or spiritual accompanier knows of potential risks when entering into a counselling or accompaniment relationship, but an awareness of the potential risks enables her to facilitate more appropriately without withholding the cathartic opportunity. Although the ethical difficulties may seem insurmountable (Gubi 2009b), practitioners whose work includes prayer have often carefully reflected on the issues (Gubi 2008, 2011b) and have reached a place of understanding of the issues where they have found the use of prayer to be less implicated with ethical dilemmas than the literature suggests.

Table 2.1: Summary of ethical difficulties of using prayer in counselling and spiritual accompaniment

Counsellor's or accompanier's process	Client's or accompanee's process
• Fear of appropriateness of personal disclosure • How authentic can the counsellor or accompanier really be? • Potential blurred boundary issues • How will prayer affect the client or accompanee? • Potential power and mutuality differential • Will prayer benefit or burden the client or accompanee? • Fear of collusion with inauthentic prayer • Prayer can inhibit the challenging of the client or accompanee • Diversion of attention away from client or accompanee to God • Countertransference issues • Issues of competency – inadequate training • Is adequate supervision available? • Possible issues of compliance with client's or accompanee's requests and words • Reliance on God v reliance on self-determination • Prayer unrecognised by insurance companies • Insufficient research to justify use • Prayer not just a technique • Danger of regarding prayer as panacea for all ills • Praying for particular outcomes inappropriate	• Fear of authentic self before God may inhibit counselling or spiritual accompaniment • Prayer can be used to deny or distort truth • Prayer can be used to avoid painful issues • Prayer can be used to manipulate the counsellor or accompanier and God • Prayer can be used to avoid listening to self • Prayer can be used to avoid challenging self • Prayer can be used to avoid taking responsibility • Compliance with counsellor's or accompanier's expectation • Transference issues • Conflictual issues with God may inhibit counselling or spiritual accompaniment if prayer is used • Prayer can be used as a defence against insight and self-understanding • Prayer can foster inappropriate intimacy • Prayer may inhibit disclosure • The client may fear judgement if prayer is used by the counsellor or spiritual accompanier, and be inhibited • Prayer can be used as a way of avoiding possible change • Prayer can be used as wish-fulfilment rather than as transcendental acceptance

Counsellor's or accompanier's process	Client's or accompanee's process
• Danger of imposing counsellor's or accompanier's values, beliefs and prayer practice on client or accompanee • Possible violation of work-setting boundaries • Need to work within client's or accompanee's religious framework which counsellor or accompanier may not subscribe to • Integrity of counsellor and accompanier may be at risk • Difficulty of knowing how to introduce prayer into the session • Prayer can detract from the immediacy of whatever the client/accompanee is experiencing in the moment • Prayer can be indirect communication with the client or accompanee • Prayer can reveal hopes and expectations for client or accompanee • Prayer can be a place to dump issues without exploration • Difficult to psychologically explore an act of reverence and mystery – different language • Prayer can create an unhealthy oedipal triangle	• Prayer can compromise client or accompanee beliefs • Prayer can be used to create a spiritual one-upmanship on the counsellor or accompanier • Prayer can be used as indirect communication with counsellor or accompanier • Prayer can foster spiritual inadequacy in the client or accompanee • Prayer can be used to foster states of magical superstition, victimhood and helplessness • Prayer can be presented as a 'quick fix', leaving the client or accompanee unable to explore ongoing pain • Prayer can dilute the counselling or accompaniment process • Prayer can be used to bypass the complexities of the counselling or accompaniment process • Prayer can be frightening or repellent if the client or accompanee is associated with strict religious or abusive upbringing • A client or accompanee who prays regularly may be reluctant for the counsellor or accompanier to use prayer if she feels that her prayer should have been enough or if she has been told that she is resisting God's grace by others

(adapted from Gubi 2009b)

How prayer is integrated ethically

The second consideration for good practice is an awareness of how prayer can be pragmatically but ethically integrated. The literature suggests that the counsellor or spiritual accompanier should conduct a formal assessment of the client's spiritual history (West 2002, 1998b; Magaletta and Brawer 1998; Richards and Bergin 1997). This enables the counsellor and spiritual accompanier to communicate an acceptance of the client's spirituality, and to gain a better sense of the client's and accompanee's world and spiritual practice. Some practitioners do formalise the use of prayer as a possible intervention, and are open in their disclosure about their spirituality. However, many counselling approaches (particularly humanistic approaches) and many spiritual accompaniers do not conduct 'formal assessments' at the contracting stage of the relationship. In such cases, practitioners use pre-contact information or a symbolic environment (often discreet religious symbols in the room or on jewellery) to communicate acceptance of spirituality. Clients and accompanees who are in touch with their own spirituality can often become aware of the counsellor's openness to spirituality through their presence, way of being and unconscious communication. This is likely to be more explicitly present with spiritual accompaniers. Instead of a formalised procedure, the integration of prayer seems to rely more on a sensitive awareness of the client's or accompanee's needs and an intuitive sensing of the appropriateness of the situation and the client/accompanee. It is likely that the counsellor or accompanier has informally gained a sense of her client's/accompanee's coping strategies and spirituality as the relationship has unfolded, so the integration of prayer is more often informed by the quality of attunement and connection between counsellor and client, and accompanier and accompanee. It is therefore more likely to be a relational and intuitive process based on an awareness of the appropriateness of prayer for the client or accompanee. Prayer must *not* be mechanistic and routine (except perhaps in the provision of silence at the beginning of the session) and must *not* be attributed to external sources (e.g. the Holy Spirit – 'I feel led by the Holy Spirit to pray…') except where such attribution actually stems from discernment that comes from the counsellor's or accompanier's conscious awareness.

The quality and characteristics of the prayer

The third consideration for good practice is an awareness of the quality and characteristics of prayer. Prayer must have a quality of naturalness about it, with the notion of prayer being introduced with the tentative quality of 'feeling your way' that emerges out of a sense of respect for the client or accompanee (e.g. 'Some people have found this helpful and I wonder if you feel it would be appropriate...'). The prayer has to feel relevant to the context and the 'moment' of what is being shared, and must not interrupt the agenda or take the client or accompanee away from experiencing the 'felt sense' of the moment. Prayer has to respect the client's or accompanee's autonomy, and attention needs to be paid to potential issues of deference and compliance (Rennie 1994). In checking out issues of deference and compliance, it is important to gain the client's consent, although to gain formal written consent, as Magaletta and Brawer (1998) suggest, might detract from the intimacy of the moment and lead to an intellectualisation of the phenomenon in which the simplicity and power of the experience is lost. It is important that the client or accompanee is able to refuse prayer, and it seems important that the counsellor or accompanier is reflexive about her clients 'never refusing prayer', to honestly ascertain if her method of introducing prayer can enable a client or accompanee to refuse. If prayer occurs with the counsellor's or accompanier's eyes closed, the practitioner may more fully engage with the prayer experience itself, but she may miss having a sense of the client's or accompanee's way of being as she prays. The use of silence at the beginning of a session may be the most appropriate form of prayer at this stage of the session as it enables the client or accompanee to gain stillness and a focus for the work. It provides a spiritual space which facilitates the client or accompanee in focusing on their 'point of pain' or on the essence of their deepest self (authenticity) which allows the unconscious to speak. The prayerful space also acknowledges the spiritual context of the work in a subtle way.

> They're sensing that I'm there for them, and the silence is not a cutting-off, it's actually a discovering for us both, where we're going to go. And certainly it feels like opening out – you can feel a settling down. And it helps them rather than sort of say how difficult it was to park, they will then come up with what it is they want to make use of their time. (Gubi 2008, p.150)

Praying with words may inhibit the expression of certain emotions. Lengthy prayer and routine, mechanistic prayer are not appropriate. Any verbal prayer needs to be focused on the client's or accompanee's needs, and be a simple acknowledgement of what they want to bring. Praying at times of desperation may take the client or accompanee away from experiencing the aloneness and the fear of the experience. However, after that has initially been experienced and explored, prayer may be beneficial at a time when the clients'/accompanees' autonomy has been diminished. Meditative prayer (or mindfulness) may also be appropriate at times when the client or accompanee is experiencing panic, as such prayer carries anxiety-reducing traits (McDonald 1999; Helminiak 1982; Shapiro 1980). The use of ritual to aid completion, resolution, a letting go and a committal can also be an appropriate place for prayer to be integrated in counselling and spiritual accompaniment.

> I had a client… [S]he had a very sad obstetric history, and she'd lost six children, and we worked through this for a few sessions, and when we came to what felt to be, towards the end, she'd actually brought baby clothes that she'd knitted for these children, and had kept for many, many years. It must have been probably about fifteen years after and she brought these clothes, and she lit a candle for each of these children, and she named them, and then we just committed them to God, with the names, into his keeping… Impossible to recall the exact words, but something like saying to God, acknowledging that these were His children and naming them and committing each of them by name to God for his keeping, and to allow the client, by name, to be able to let them go into His care… I would say that from that time she was much more at peace about this…she was in a far more peaceful frame of mind, a happier frame of mind, when we completed the work… It really felt as if it had been completed, and I think that was the last time the children were mentioned. (Gubi 2008, p.159)

However, it is important that the client or accompanee does not expect instant healing from the ritual, but is able to continue to work on the issues as and when they recur. It is also important that the counsellor/ accompanier checks out that the client/accompanee does not feel that the counsellor/accompanier would be disappointed if healing or closure did not occur. This can enhance the client's/accompanee's authenticity. Christian practices such as the 'laying on of hands' and 'speaking in tongues' are rare. However, they do occur and are existentially powerful to those who encounter them. It is important that this type of ritual is not routine or mechanistic, and that the counsellor/accompanier reflects carefully on her need to introduce such practice. Again, such practice needs to have a sense of naturalness about it for both counsellor/accompanier and client/accompanee. It also needs to emerge from a discernment of the 'felt sense' of the moment.

Silence that fosters a connectedness to the sacred (Pargament 1997; Ulanov and Ulanov 1982) is a less controversial but nevertheless overt use of prayer.

> I think the silence gives people an opportunity, and because I believe in Grace... I do think that if I/they can find a way in which to stop for a moment, and become willing, it's that saying 'yes' again, even if it's at a not completely conscious level, that that allows something else to happen, and that's the bit that's beyond us, really... It kind of opens a door somewhere... I don't know – it is the touch of God. I mean, I do believe – a part of me, I have to say it that way, there is a part of me that believes that the grand being, God, whatever words I use, is active in some sense, not simply a large process of which we are all a part. There's another part of me that believes that, but there is a part of me that believes that there are moments when I know it in my own life – the finger of God touches you, and the experience of that is sometimes a conscious experience, a knowledge of being graced, of being blessed, and sometimes not. (Gubi 2008, p.149)

Although prayer has the potential to disempower the client/accompanee, prayer also has the potential to empower the client/accompanee. This can be seen in the client/accompanee taking responsibility for the praying, in the way that the content of prayer changes over time, and in the ability of the client/accompanee to ask for prayer. All of these can be regarded as signs of developing autonomy. Some of the common uses of prayer in counselling or accompaniment are at the end of a session or at the termination of working relationship. Using prayer at these times is less intrusive to the process of the session. This use of prayer to convey messages of hope and affirmation reinforces the work in which the client/accompanee has responsibility for healing, change and/or acceptance. Prayer for intervention that introduces connotations of magic (e.g. instant healing and miracles), victimhood and helplessness is not appropriate. Using prayer to end the working relationship can act as a way of consolidating the gain (Dobbins 2000), enabling closure and termination of the work at both a practical and a spiritual level.

Issues of tension and difficulty for the counsellor or spiritual accompanier

The fourth consideration for good practice is an awareness of the possible areas of tension and difficulty for the counsellor or accompanier. Prayer should not be used to impose or communicate the counsellor's or accompanier's values to the client/accompanee (Magaletta and Brawer 1998; McMinn 1996; Rose 2002; Webster 1992) because the client/accompanee may be unable to challenge what is being prayed, and the use of prayer in this way is open to manipulation and abuse. However, values that are compatible with the counselling or accompaniment values (e.g. the client is a person of worth and of value) may be appropriately imparted and sanctified through prayer.

> So we place all this in the hands of God knowing that on your own you feel really weak and vulnerable, even though there are lots of indications of your tremendous growth and seriously working on yourself, trying to integrate your past and become a more wholesome and worthwhile person, although in many of our lives you are already that. So we finish the session by saying thank you God, for Johnny. Amen. (Gubi 2008, p.184)

Prayer may also be a useful medium through which the client/accompanee is more able to hear the counsellor's/accompanier's insight and awareness of the client/accompanee and of their process. Rather than being an indirect communication with the client/accompanee, which may be regarded as the antithesis of counselling (Gubi 2001), prayer can be regarded as a direct communication with the client/accompanee if God is at the centre of the client/accompanee. In my previous research (Gubi 2008), some counsellors were reluctant to enable their client to explore their motivation for, and act of, praying. However, if prayer is to be integrated into counselling practice, it must not be treated any differently from any other intervention in counselling. Exploration of whatever happens is an implicit part of therapy, and prayer is no different. The interview data revealed that some counsellors explored the client's need to pray before the prayer. Others waited and let the exploration happen in a natural and unobtrusive way. Others explored the client's process after the prayer. Out of respect for the client, it was important to travel alongside the client through the prayer (even if the content did not feel comfortable for the counsellor), and then to therapeutically unpick the process, or appropriately challenge the client by sensitively, congruently, but tentatively sharing the counsellor's insights and awareness of the client to further therapeutic exploration. There is no evidence that I can find of how spiritual accompaniers handle prayer in similar situations, but if prayer is to be used, it must not assume a 'sacredness' that excludes it from the way that other interventions are worked with, even though some (e.g. McMinn 1996) consider that prayer is different from other interventions.

Self-disclosure of the counsellor's spirituality was also identified as an area of potential tension. This may be less problematic for spiritual accompaniers – but it is important not to assume this. Disclosure of the counsellor's or accompanier's spirituality can enable a more profound connection for clients/accompanees who want to explore spiritual issues, because exploring spiritual material is often problematic for clients (West 2000, 2002). However, the sharing of spiritual beliefs may lead to an unhelpful transference phenomenon (Hinksman 1999) or inappropriately influence the counselling/accompaniment agenda.

Supervision issues

For counsellors, bringing issues of prayer to supervision is highly problematic, and many counsellors do not feel free to explore their practice of prayer because of a fear of not being understood; fear of being judged; fear of losing respect and credibility; fear of being thought of as transgressing; fear of exposure by the supervisor; lack of trust in how the supervisor will treat the disclosure; fear of condemnation and dismissal of something that is important and precious to the counsellor (Gubi 2007). However, it is equally important for both counsellors and spiritual accompaniers that prayer is discussed in supervision, even when some accompaniers might regard it as 'normal practice'.

Concluding comments

Prayer is no more problematic than other counselling interventions, nor should it be treated any differently from any other therapeutic intervention within the context of counselling and psychotherapy. In both counselling and spiritual accompaniment, prayer needs to be approached with a knowledge and awareness of the possible ethical difficulties, and be integrated in a manner that is respecting of, and enhancing of, the client's/accompanee's autonomy, and in a way that fosters the client's/accompanee's well-being. There is an assumption in counselling that 'secular' interventions are acceptable and that spiritual interventions are less acceptable. Yet all counselling interventions are to some degree problematic and need the same degree of careful ethical consideration. The same is true for spiritual accompaniment. No intervention must be regarded as a panacea for all ills, even though it is possible to gain that sense of a panacea about prayer from some writers (e.g. Ten Eyck 1993). To regard prayer in this way can be disrespecting of the client/accompanee. If prayer can be empowering, then arguably it is unethical to withhold it (Gubi 2002) if the client/accompanee has a healthy spirituality, and prayer is an important part of their spirituality (Richards and Bergin 1997). If the counsellor/accompanier also shares that spirituality and is cautious in her approach and in her awareness of her client/accompanee, then the process should be open to any intervention (or 'mode of relating') that can enhance the client's/accompanee's growth (depending on how 'growth' is psychologically and spiritually defined) and enable the alliance to deepen relationally.

The purpose of this chapter has not been to advocate the use of prayer, but it is important for counselling to become open to the use of spiritual interventions, such as prayer, which can be utilised for the benefit of the client. It is equally important for spiritual accompaniers not to take the use of prayer for granted and treat it as a 'norm' because that is what happens in other areas of Christian practice. The integration of prayer is intrinsically pragmatic and has to be characterised by an openness and acceptance of what is meaningful to the other. These qualities are not always evident in counselling and supervision, and need further examination at a personal level, and advancement at a cultural level in relation to working with the spiritual dimension of counselling.

Chapter 3

Creative Methods in Spiritual Exploration

Inviting the Sublime into the Room

Phil Goss

She watched the sky, imagining her mother, whom she had not seen for two years, returning on every aeroplane which passed across the sky. She often thought she heard the sound of her mother's voice calling out her name – *'Lee-anne, Lee-anne'* – in amongst the low drone of the engines. One day, she was sure she had seen the vapour trail behind one plane float free and form straight white lines and curling loops against a bright blue sky, in a combination which looked just like *'lee'* – the affectionate nickname her mum had used for her. Somehow this last memory, from her seventh year, seemed to have stayed with her so vividly, that now, in her fiftieth year, when she closed her eyes, the letters in the *'lee'* shape had become a deep hue of velvety gold surrounded by a distant, but ebbing, light which gave her such a mysterious feeling of connection – not just to her mother, but to something much bigger, much more powerful than the long-lost person whose disappearance had wrenched the heart out of the young girl…

> For some people, discovering higher (or deeper) consciousness and spirituality happens in a moment of revelation. For others it is a long, steady process of opening and unfolding, of becoming aware of forces beyond the self. (Rogers 1993, p.200)

Don moved slowly through transitions. For this man, all the significant events of his life seemed to have happened in slow motion. First, there was the loss of his friends and the familiarity of, not to mention spiritual connection to, the place he had grown up in when his family had moved from one part of the country to another, when he was 13. Second, the death of his stepfather whom he had grown to love after initially resenting his presence, when the young man was 16, and the attendant loss of his religious faith in the face of the seemingly random nature of life and death. Third, his partner leaving him when he was 30. In each case, the stand-out memories and dreams about the events concerned moved through his mind's eye at a snail's pace: his mum's car bumping slowly against the curb as it left the village he had grown up in; then later, her mouth taking an age to open as she told Don his stepdad had died; and finally his partner gradually shutting the garden gate, and staring with his empty, unloving eyes back at Don, as if their once passionate relationship had never existed. Why was it that something inside him seemed to need to move slowly through big changes, as if telling him to slow down and notice what was *really* important? But what was 'important' – or was all of this…all of this life…meaningless, as he often told himself; partly at least to stop all the hurt consuming him like the huge beast which he had dreamt more than once was about to swallow him whole.

The focus of this chapter is on the ways in which the spiritual intersects with creativity to generate insights via therapeutically based interventions which can be applied to a range of allied contexts such as spiritual accompaniment and spiritual direction. My aim is to offer some ideas and themes which will be of value, or at least of some interest, for anyone working with people who want to see and know more clearly what is at work within and around them. In the disguised examples above, two people turn to counselling and psychotherapy for help in making sense of associations, images and feelings which may have a spiritual aspect. This aspect reflects a search for meaning and insight which goes beyond the relational, empirical and purely personal spheres of experience. Using these two examples, supported by discussion which draws on thinking about the principles and application of creative and expressive methods, I will argue for the importance of recognising the bridge between creativity and spirituality. This bridge, I suggest, operates at a level in the human psyche that makes available powerful individual, collective and spiritual resources which can generate invaluable meanings and growth for all of us, and particularly for clients who may need our help in finding their way forward (I will use 'client' as a catch-all term for the purposes of this discussion).

In this context, the use of 'spiritual' is offered in its broader sense, to encompass any exploratory process which endeavours to gain insight into the depths of human experience. It therefore includes such processes of individual or collaborative exploration in any field of human endeavour where this may happen, formal or informal, whether named 'spiritual', 'religious' or neither.

By 'creative methods', I am referring to a range of approaches that have sprung up in the last 70 years or so for accessing what may lie outside conscious awareness but which is waiting to come forward to provide insight and healing. It is crucial to highlight from the outset the importance of only embarking on creative activities which we feel competent, confident and suitably well supported, by some form of appropriate supervision, to offer the person we are working with – not least because these activities can unleash powerful feelings which need a safe container. Training in art, drama, music and other creative therapies provides the opportunity to secure this aspect in depth. However, it is still possible to offer interventions which can augment forms of spiritually related process, drawing on these approaches, as long as we are properly supported and do not step beyond our limits of practice competence.

These approaches are based around deep cultural, religious and artistic traditions which go back thousands of years, and which also recognise the creative and healing power of arts, such as visual art, dance, drama, music and literature. Carl Jung, the founder of analytical psychology, saw the symbolic importance of these as avenues into working with the unconscious, including where this overlaps with what we might mean by the 'spiritual', and the importance of us each finding the medium through which we can best do this. For him, this included a kind of imaginative play with the stones and rocks of the shores of Lake Zurich (Jung 1989) as a way of unlocking the symbolic interplay between unconscious influences in him and his active capacity to make meaningful sense of these. Contemporary, post-Jungian writing has further developed these ideas around using art as a vehicle for healing and development (e.g. Matthews 2015).

Later, Carl Rogers (1961) wrote of the importance of symbolisation of feelings as a way to get behind unhelpful conceptions of self. His daughter, Natalie Rogers (1993), developed ways of working creatively in therapy, drawing on both of these influences. This bridge between Jungian and person-centred notions of creative and symbolic expression will be drawn on to elucidate further ways of applying such principles to spiritual exploration.

In support of this, I want to lay out the foundations of my therapeutic approach as a Jungian analyst who often works in a relational-integrative way with adults and young people, incorporating humanistic and person-centred principles in my practice. My model for working is based on the perception of there being four main archetypes of experience activated in the therapeutic encounter (and therefore, by default, I would argue this applies likewise in the relational encounter of spiritual direction and accompaniment). By archetypes, I mean elusive but present 'essences' which exist across the natural order and are within human experience, operating under the surface of conscious awareness in all cultures, and stretching back across our collective history, operating on a continuum which arises through human instinct and is represented in common images which are activated in a spectrum of human activities (Jung 1968). An example would be the archetype of 'hero' which is represented in arts and culture across all human societies. This archetype can also be activated in reality by individual human beings who do remarkable feats which earn them the respect, or even idealisation, of the community around them. The instinct to be heroic resides in all of us, but it needs to be activated by external events or internal drivers (or both) before it becomes realised. This potentiality of archetypes is also bipolar, as there is a negative correlate to the positive – so for the 'hero' archetype, an opposite correlate could be 'coward', 'victim' or 'bad guy', or some other archetype of weakness, failure or evil. Again, these archetypes only become 'real' when they are activated in, or by, us.

This principle informs my therapeutic frame of reference. This reflects an integrative continuum in which I work as a psychotherapist, and stretches and moves according to the needs of clients and my sense of how to respond to these. I perceive there to be four main archetypes of the therapeutic (or other pastoral/helping) encounter: relationship, healing, meaning and creativity. These are archetypal in that the potential for them is present in every properly grounded piece of therapeutic (and pastoral/spiritually focused) work between two (or more) people. However, there is also the potential for the opposite, darker and sometimes damaging side of the archetype to constellate in the therapeutic space. So, where the positive archetype of relationship in the therapeutic space is activated, then psychological contact, trust and warmth are present, for example. Where the negative pole is activated, then contact is faulty, intermittent or absent, and mistrust and even hostility might be present, with all the challenges inherent in this. However, such a challenge can provide the potential to work this through to produce something of great value for the client; in Jungian terms, working with *shadow* (Samuels, Shorter and Plaut 1986, p.138) in order to find what hidden possibilities and potentialities may be locked within it, awaiting release.

As you will have noticed, there is an explicitly transpersonal (Rowan 2005) dimension to my work. I find this term helpful in how it captures the sense that there is more going on between psychotherapist and client than what is present in the 'here and now' dialogue between them, and in the unconscious personal projections and affect passing between them. Although in my practice noticing transference process is important in getting beneath the surface of what is going on for the client, there is also, I have found, often another fertile space present within and alongside the alchemy of conscious and unconscious communication. In this space, a dynamic can operate which facilitates change and growth that does not 'belong' to either therapist or client, nor even just to the relationship between the two. Jung (1968) had a helpful way of characterising this, when he said it is the *numinous* which catalyses meaningful insight and change in the therapeutic encounter. In other words, there has to be constellated a sense of something deeply particular to each 'I–Thou' encounter (Buber 1970) in the therapeutic or equivalent space, which in turn provides for something mysterious and powerful (or 'numinous') to be present. This enables meaningful change and/or insight to be spontaneously facilitated. Young-Eisendrath (2004, pp.184–185), a Jungian writer, characterises a consequence of working with the numinous, which can be drawn out of the individual, and which is relevant to our discussion, as 'the unconscious striving for spiritual development'.

It is valuable to note in this quotation the inherent emphasis on something both prospective and creative at work within the human psyche towards 'spiritual development' as part of what, in Jungian terms, might be seen as the 'individuation process' – that is, the journey towards becoming who we fully are (Jung 1953), but which can also be seen in terms of the actualising tendency in person-centred language (Rogers 1961), and in a variety of expressions relating to development and fulfilment in different spiritual and religious traditions.

Creativity, therapy and spirituality

So, if forward-looking, generative and creative forces are at work in the human psyche alongside those influences that can get us into stuck, confused and even destructive patterns, how might we see these operating within, or alongside, our 'spiritual' sense of self, whatever that may mean to us each as individuals? In the disguised vignettes introduced at the start of this chapter, which we will return to later, *individuality* is key, as I believe it to be in all processes of healing and growth.

We find our creativity, I would argue, via our sense of individuality, and we do so only if we are in touch with something that is elementally 'us', which may give us a sense of meaning that some might call 'spiritual' (although others may use a term such as 'existential'). Our individuality, our 'I' – whether we experience that in a singular or pluralistic form, or both – is activated when we are creative (and vice versa: our creativity arises where our 'I' is activated), and I want to highlight its significance for spiritual exploration. One more observation I would like to make draws on the polarities portrayed within the archetypal level of therapeutic practice set out above: it is important to remain aware of the presence of *destructiveness* wherever creativity shows itself.

The energy that gets locked, blocked and exploded out, via destructive patterns of behaviour and relationship, towards others or ourselves, can often be key to unlocking creative expression and process, as I will illustrate. Working with destructive forces presenting in the person we are working with, and where this shows itself in our work with them, is a key component in releasing creativity which has an essentially spiritual quality. Destructiveness could be seen as an expression of a spiritual hunger for healing and psychological balance which has been turned on its head because of how stymied and split the creative side of the person has become. One is the flip side of the other, and therefore both deserve equal respect and attention in our work, in order to allow for where destructive influences demand expression before something creative can be found, and where the former can be channelled into some meaningful activity or expression – 'sublimated' to use Freud's term (Freud 1961) for describing how potentially destructive libido can find healthy expression (e.g. where anger or desire is channelled into artistic, cultural or sporting activity).

Our interest, though, is primarily in a kind of 'spiritual libido' which creative methods can access and draw out. This idea has its roots in the disputes between Freud and Jung, with the former, of course, advocating the exclusively psychosexual nature of libido, whereas Jung thought there was more to this, and saw libido as taking differing forms. This would depend on what may be happening for a person, including their stage of life, and involve *creative* and *destructive* manifestations of libidinal energies. On the basis of his extensive analytic work with people in the second half of life, Jung concluded that it was common for libido to evolve from more overtly sexual, or relational, forms in earlier life towards something more spiritual (Goss 2015). This corresponds with his principle of individuation: the psyche orienting itself towards a more reflective and introspective stance ahead of the end of life.

My use of the term 'destructive' can, on the surface, be seen as a description of something that is 'wrong' with you or me – something about the enactment of sometimes dangerously immature aspects of ourselves which we might inadvertently inflict on ourselves or others. Of course, it can – and, not uncommonly, *does* – refer to something like this – where a careless or hostile word or action brings about damage or suffering, for example. However, there is a sense in which destructiveness, like creativity, can act as an agent by itself, generating damage and suffering from outside our conscious awareness of its intent. Serious illness, natural disaster or unexpected life events, however tangentially or otherwise linked to any part we may have played, generally fit into this category. The historical notion of the *sublime*, like the concept of the *numinous,* highlights the way we can be affected by powerful experiences in terrifying or awe-inspiring ways (or both), but with more of an emphasis on the aesthetic quality of how we perceive, and receive, these (Shaw 2006) – hence making it a valuable term to hold in mind when working with creative methods. This idea of the sublime, as holding both creative and destructive archetypal energies, captures the way very difficult experiences can floor us, but also how the sometimes overwhelming nature of suffering puts us in touch with the 'I' as described above. As Bridges (2015, p.87) vividly puts it, 'Some of our most authentic moments are…those of greatest pain – moments when we feel raw, exposed and acutely vulnerable; the startling and sobering realisation that this pain is inescapably ours.' It is also possible to describe painful, destructive influences in terms of the constellation, or coming together, of a *complex* (Samuels *et al.* 1986), whereby a combination of past environmental, personality and externally present factors are melded together by powerful archetypal forces, to really hammer home, and sustain, suffering. I will give examples of working creatively with this in our case studies. So, in the same way that we may get closer to the 'I' (or 'I's) in us through working with our creativity, we can also do so through encountering pain, suffering and destructiveness. The challenge lies in how we might work with this – and the place of spirituality and meaning-making is, I contend, pivotal for providing the conditions conducive to the effectiveness of such work. As Thorne (2012) rightly points out, spirituality can be said to go beyond psychology, although I would argue the two have to be intimately linked as they both refer to inner process and its outward expression. His point, however, that the mysterious depths that are inherent in spiritual experience make finding the language to adequately capture what 'it' is, difficult, is valid. What perhaps is less tricky, but still demands careful thought, is identifying the conditions needed for growthful, creative work in this area.

Conditions for fostering creativity in spiritual exploration

Where spirituality is given its due place in the work we are doing in therapeutic, pastoral or spiritual accompaniment/direction contexts, the person we are working with is given, often unconsciously, a sense of permission to explore fully their personal and spiritual journey. Where it is not, we are leaving something fundamental out of the equation, and the impact can be subtly, but crucially, damaging. Pargament (2007) gives a useful example of this when he describes hearing someone who has both priestly and clinical responsibilities tell of the way they leave their pastoral role and religious beliefs outside the door before working therapeutically, and the dulling effect this tends to have on meaningful, creative therapeutic work. This approach, though not to be confused with the need to sometimes make important ethical decisions about disclosure to the client, reiterates the importance of the principle of not leaving parts of ourselves, as practitioners, 'outside the room'. If we are not fully present to our spirituality (and our own creativity, not to mention destructive tendencies), the client will be more likely to find it very difficult to be present to their own. This, in turn, rests on our capacity to recognise, and allow in, what

Harborne (2012, p.4) describes as our connection to 'something…
greater than ourselves, and which we recognise through personal
experience'. Where we hold our relationship to this in awareness, we
also – crucially – create and sustain a container for the client to be able
to validate their own connections and experiences in this respect. This
way, spirituality – or what Swinton (2001, p.20) calls 'the outward
expression of the inner workings of the human spirit' – can truly have
its place in our work, and the container we have created for the client
truly becomes *creative*. This also allows for the presence of *destructive*
energies to be contained, manifested and portrayed via creative and
artistic (in the broadest sense) expression – a crucial component in
facilitating all facets of spiritual exploration.

Two further valuable reference points for working with elements
arising from outside our usual conscious field of awareness, including
where this has a spiritual resonance, are Jung's (1968) notion of
the collective unconscious and Henri Corbin's (1972) concept
of the *mundus imaginalis*. Both men identified commonalities of deep
human experiencing which are available to us – Jung's discovery being
that beneath the individuality of our personal unconscious, with its
repository of repressed memories and instincts that are unique to
each of us, there lies a reservoir of shared imagery, and instinctual
and emotional experience which ranges across cultures and the
whole of human history. As Stevens (2005) puts it, 'we are all two
million years old'. This reservoir is available to all of us, in the form
of archetypally charged imagery and bodily based instincts, which can
be symbolised in our imagination, dreams and – crucially – structured
creative activities which provide access to them. Corbin (1972),
on the other hand, provides a powerful model for how *image*, such
a pivotal element in creative therapeutic and allied work, becomes
available to us. The 'imaginal world', he posits, resides in each of
us, just below the ordinary level of consciousness, and is a vibrant
layer of psyche which spontaneously generates images in response to
sensory input. So, I experience something – a sudden blast of wind
on a hillside, say – and, as I steady my feet on the path, an image of
a bird tumbling sideways flashes across my mind's eye, and is then
gone. I cannot put my finger on where this image is from (a mix of real
and televisual experiences, probably). However, it is the combination
of the instinctual reaction to the sensory input from that which is
experienced as sudden, prompted by a blast of the wind, and the

immediate availability of imagery from the *mundus imaginalis* that brings the image into awareness. So here we have a valuable explanation for *how* symbolic imagery becomes available for us to work creatively, drawing on archetypal imagery and themes (in my case, the bird could, I speculate, represent vulnerabilities and fears about being 'knocked off balance' in life, as well as the growth that can occur when we make ourselves vulnerable).

As far as working in an explicitly creative way with clients is concerned, Natalie Rogers (1993) helpfully augments her father's (Carl's) identification of two conditions which correspond to the principles for working with spirituality that I have been outlining above. These conditions are:

1. *Psychological safety:* This involves offering a containing and empathic context in which the client can freely explore and express their feelings and thoughts, boundaried by the application of fundamental ethical principles such as autonomy, confidentiality and non-maleficence (BACP 2016).

2. *Psychological freedom:* This refers to the facilitation of the client's capacity to form symbolic expression of feelings, which a person may be consciously aware of, but otherwise believe it is not safe or allowable for them to express – or which may lie outside conscious awareness, waiting to find a suitable form of conscious expression. This latter idea corresponds well with Jung's (1970) definition for a symbol as 'an intuitive idea that cannot yet be formulated in any other or better way'. So here the symbol (such as a spontaneously forming image) presents us with what is waiting to come into conscious awareness and seeks form in order to express a feeling, or is perhaps alerting us in a compensatory way to what we are otherwise not noticing or avoiding. Our role as facilitators is to convey a genuine sense of permission to the client for this to happen, however shameful, fearful or destructive the hidden feelings or influences might be.

3. *Offering stimulating and challenging experiences:* Natalie Rogers' further condition recognises that, as facilitators of the client's creative exploration of their spirituality, we need to take a more overtly active role than the usual facilitation stance of

face-to-face therapeutic or accompaniment/direction work. As she puts it herself, verbal interaction is simply not enough to enable the potential in creative-expressive methods to be realised: 'Since our culture is particularly geared to verbalizing, it is necessary to stimulate the client…by offering experiences that challenge her' (Rogers 1993, p.17).

By 'challenge', I also take this to mean 'wake something up' in the client. In my experience, there is almost always something 'there', just out of our awareness waiting to show itself, and it is as if we are asleep (unconscious?) to its presence, although we may sense something is present (e.g. an image, a word, a sound) but just out of reach. Our role in this sense is to provide the intervention/activity which will 'wake up', in the client, the potential to notice, receive and work with what is there. This can be done effectively in an entirely relational, warm and even gentle way.

Rogers (1993, p.17) emphasises the value of structured activities as she goes on to say, 'Carefully planned experiments, or experiences, designed to involve the individual in the expressive arts (if she chooses to take the opportunity) help her focus on the process of creating.' Here the principles of pure person-centred, non-directive practice are placed into the background in order to provide the structured activity which will release the feeling and allow the insight that is awaiting expression in the individual we are working with. In my view, this is truly person-centred, as it places the client at the centre of our focus as we draw on our feeling, thinking, intuiting and sensation functions (to refer to Jung's (1970) typological frame of reference) to get a sense of what creative activity might be helpful for the client. Needless to say, this requires a developed reflective capacity on the part of the practitioner, in order to get in touch with what seems to be emerging for the client. In this respect, the depth of our personal and, in the context of this discussion, spiritual development will be pivotal to our capacity to attune to where the client 'is'.

The final principle to briefly set out is around the structuring of creative activities. Kolb's (1984) experiential learning cycle – of concrete experience, reflective observation abstract conceptualisation and active experimentation – provides, in my experience, a consistently helpful framework for them. I offer the client a concrete experience (e.g. the invitation to explore the properties of a stone which they select from a spread of stones on the floor). I invite them to reflect on any observations or connections arising (e.g. they may notice a connection with a feeling such as isolation, arising from experiencing the coldness on touching the stone). I allow them to further reflect and consider this connection, and come to a more fully formed, though not definitive, conclusion about the meaning(s) arising (e.g. 'My closer relationships still leave me sometimes with a feeling of isolation'), and then, finally, I invite them to consider where to take this next ('Would you, maybe, like to do a bit of free writing on what this has brought up, or you could draw with these crayons?'), thus allowing them to restart the cycle, slightly closer in to the heart of the matter. This approach can fit spiritual themes well. Kolb's cycle is not a perfect fit, in my view, as it does not take sufficiently into account the surprising breakthroughs into awareness of previously unconscious material (including spiritually charged material) which can happen at any point in a creative-therapeutic activity or cycle. However, it does provide a suitable vehicle to enable meaningful circumambulation in creative activities which facilitate spiritual exploration.

Jung (1989) spoke of the value of circumambulation, which means to keep going around something to know it better, as fully as possible – for example, revisiting all aspects of a dream: carefully looking at each part of it as well as the whole; looking at it from all angles, to get as full a picture of the meaning(s) conveyed by it as possible.

Now I will turn to apply the principles outlined – and describe the methods deployed – to the two therapeutic vignettes, which are a disguised amalgam from spiritually focused, creative aspects of my practice.

Leanne

The theme of loss, if not trauma, suggests itself even from the brief glimpse into Leanne's formative experiences of life – in particular, her mother disappearing when she was eight after saying she was 'going on holiday'. I experienced a strong sense of unavailability and distance in her way of being (suggesting something was split off and dissociated), as well as the presence of something 'frozen' in the room. In the first couple of sessions, I noticed a certain coldness in the room, and there was a moment when a shiver passed through me, starting in my feet and racing up my legs and upper body to my forehead, making me momentarily dizzy – as if I had suddenly been encased in ice. The moment soon passed, but left me with a stark (but helpful) image of Leanne, and of me, encased in a huge slab of ice. I also had a growing sense of something else stuck in the ice alongside the two of us – something emanating from the depths, which was bigger than and 'other' to us. This intuiting of a transpersonal, spiritual dimension to the work made me wonder if this might be key to her process, and the unblocking of her grieving (Bright 2000). I am always careful in my psychotherapeutic practice to check out closely whether or not creative methods are appropriate for the client and their needs. It is easy, especially when things get stuck or difficult, to reach into my creative-expressive tool box and suggest an activity to get closer to what is happening, when it is not uncommon for clients to simply need to sit with difficult feelings (or with their difficulty in accessing them), in order to notice them and be able to engage at some level with them. In this case, though, it became clear to me that something in Leanne had become unreachable and closed off, as if behind a locked door – and the key had been thrown away. We had completed seven weekly sessions, and when I floated the idea with my supervisor of doing something more actively creative, she expressed a feeling of relief, as if we had been frozen in supervision too. I felt it as well, realising it was hard to envisage the ice melting in the face-to-face attempt to foster relational depth (Mearns and Cooper 2005) which is standard to counselling and psychotherapy practice. I began by offering Leanne the opportunity to draw. ('…it may be a way to get closer to what you said you cannot feel anymore.' To make it clear, the idea would be that she does not think about what she is drawing – she simply doodles on a large sheet of paper, using whatever pens, crayons and chalks she might choose from the selection.) She seemed a bit puzzled by the idea, so I asked her to think about it, and that it was fine if she did not want to. She started to smile and then stopped herself before saying, 'But I was rubbish at art in school, and the teachers always told me my pictures weren't very good.' This is a familiar response, and it is important to stress to clients how what is being suggested is a way of helping them express what is going on for them, and nothing to do with the 'quality' of what they produce. The risk in suggesting arts-based activity in the therapeutic, or allied, space is that it locks the client back into that feeling of 'I'm not good enough', and closes possibility down. However, this situation also provides an opportunity to explore what such a condition of worth (Rogers 1961) is about –

for example, 'I will only be accepted (and loved) if my drawing is good enough' – and enables the person to free themselves to be truer to self.

The following week, Leanne came back and said she wanted to try the doodle drawing. The activity that I offered her drew on a combination of Natalie Rogers' (1993) 'big doodle' activity and Violet Oaklander's (2007) 'scribble' activity. It involved a concrete experience of being asked to close her eyes and doodle in the air, crayons in hand (I noticed this might be a potentially powerful parallel to her image of the vapour trails in the sky, although this was not a deliberate link – Rogers suggests this anyway – as it is important to keep the whole process open and neutral for the client to develop as they choose, or find themselves doing). Then I invited her to doodle on the paper, filling as much or as little of it as she wished to. After about three minutes, I asked her if she had doodled enough. She said she had, so I invited her to open her eyes and in her own time, and as Oaklander (2007) suggests, just look at the paper filled with scribble and allow images to form in the curls, spaces and crossed lines in front of her. What happened next was profound. Leanne told me that doing this reminded her of when she was a child. She would lie on the grass, sometimes by herself, but sometimes with her mother, and stare up at the clouds. Shapes and images would form – dinosaur heads, cars, flowers and so on – and when she was with her mother she would tell her what she was seeing, and her mother would do the same. Leanne paused, and, with her eyes welling up with tears, she said that she had just remembered one time when they played a game in which they both had to say simultaneously what they were seeing – and they both said 'Our house!' at the same time. She broke down, and a long flood of tearful feelings came up in heavy sobs from a deep, deep place in her. When this passed, she said, 'I want to see the sky', so we both went to the window and looked up into the grey, overcast sky. After a few minutes of silence, her eyes widened and she said, 'I can see it…I can see it again…the house…our house…it's glowing…' Then a minute or so later, '…it's fading…it's gone.' She turned to me and said, 'Thank you… I've found her again… Not sure, but maybe I've found myself again…' The session was coming to a close, so I checked if there was anything else she needed to do (e.g. notice what was happening in her body, what of her could still be 'up in the sky' and what 'on the ground') to re-ground herself in reality (an important thing always to check after using creative approaches to ensure the client can go securely back to day-to-day activity). She indicated she was OK, and we brought the session to a close back on our chairs.

From here, although the ice continued for some weeks to melt only now and again, it was clear something important had happened. Through the activity, Leanne had contacted a powerful memory which brought her closer to her attachment to her mother, and helped her explore her grief, releasing the trapped energy in the grip of her 'lost mother complex'. In Jungian language, her underlying self had been activated through a *numinous experience* – activated, one could say, via a *sublimely aesthetic* experience of image, which clearly had a spiritual as well as personal dimension to it. The symbol of house/home can be seen to represent our self-as-home (or *temenos*), and there was a sense that Leanne was now back in touch with her deeper self/selves. This then facilitated a fuller process of self-discovery, over time, which she reported had got her in touch with her underlying 'path through life' as well as reactivating her link with her mother.

Don

It turned out Don's struggle with the task of discovering what his life might really be 'for' had a more explicitly religious underpinning, in the sense of him needing a container which was 'bigger than him' for making sense of the series of losses, and changes, that he had experienced. These seemed, he said, to have 'torn a layer off me, one by one, until there was almost nothing left'. The most recent 'layer' had been torn away when his partner of four years, Stuart, had left him, telling him he could not see 'anything in you [Don] which would make me want to stay'. This cruel judgement seemed, to Don, to be further compounded by the fact that his partner was a priest; Don had been surprised to notice that he liked the feeling of moving vicariously closer back towards the Church through getting into the relationship with Stuart, and the way his, and their, gay sexuality seemed generally to be comfortably accepted by the church community which Don became a part of, until the relationship abruptly ended.

As highlighted in the opening portrayal of Don, the theme of 'motion through time' seemed pivotal. All memories of crucial points of departure in his life seemed to be played out in front of him, in slow motion, in reverie and dreams, so that 'it feels like life is trying to torture me…rubbing it in my face'. After a number of sessions exploring this theme and not seeming to get far with it at all, I noticed a restlessness in my body – my legs and feet were twitching, particularly when I was in the room with him – which also, I observed, showed itself in his bodily activity – a frantic swinging of his right leg, while he was describing his experiences, including the 'slow motion' memories in particular. After consulting with my supervisor, I decided to offer Don an activity based around both his 'body' and his 'story', using guided meditation as well as sculpting – a way of allowing a person to see a meaningful image, or theme, embodied and laid out before them (Jennings 1998) – as it seemed to me that his struggle was one with finding his place 'in time', so he could recalibrate his relationship to others, to the world and to his search for deeper meaning. I said to him, 'We could try a different way of working involving you focusing on your body as a way of understanding the story of your life better.' Don seemed to leap at this opportunity ('Yes, I'm up for that!'), and I was momentarily taken aback by his enthusiasm which seemed charged with relief. First, I suggested that he simply relax in his chair, close his eyes and notice what was happening around his body (to let go of any muscle tension, follow his breath, etc.) – a kind of guided meditation. Second, I asked him to allow an image of himself to form, and explore it ('What shape is it?', 'If it's a living thing, what is it doing?', 'Is it trying to say anything to you, and if so what?', etc.). After asking him to circumambulate ('walk right round') it in his mind one last time, I invited him to notice what was happening in his body again (to re-ground him), open his eyes and come back into our shared space. I asked him if he felt like sharing the image with me. He nodded and was clearly ready to burst out and tell me immediately. I lifted my open hand a little in a gentle 'wait' gesture and he stilled, staring at me quizzically. I said, 'Before we talk about it, I want to offer you a choice to help you really make the most of this image. You could either draw it with the crayons, pencils, chalks and paper I have here, or we could use sculpting. This is where you are the sculptor, and I become the image so you can see it in real life, right in front of you. You tell me what shape to get into (there's no physical contact) – where to put my arms, head, legs, etc., whether I stay seated or stand up, what expression to make with my face, and so on. Sometimes people find it helps to see it this way, in another person, but drawing it can be powerful too, so it's up to you.' Nodding quickly, he asked me if I could go down on to the floor and 'curl up in a ball in front of your chair, but with your head leaning against it, staring up to the ceiling'. I duly obliged, and, after a moment's silence, a chilling sound rose out of him, charged with rage, low-pitched at first, then rising higher before he shouted, 'It's killed me…it's fucking killed me!' He then collapsed back into his chair, gulping tearfully. I came out of the sculpt and sat back in my chair. I let him know I was there and present for him, and checked with him if he was OK and whether wanted to talk about this or just sit quietly. He slowed his breathing down and then started talking, explaining that the image had been of a small, iconic medal, portraying St Christopher, carrying the boy-child Jesus Christ on his shoulders, across a raging river to safety. The medal had been on a chain and had been a gift from his mother, and it carried personal as well as religious significance, as it had apparently belonged to his real father, whom he had never seen (he had left the family home when Don was very small).

'The chain was your body on the floor…and your head was the medal… I lost it when my stepdad died…actually…I threw it away, threw it in the river…cos I knew it would sink. I knew the story about St Christopher carrying Jesus across the river was a load of crap. There's nothing…nothing to carry us through this life; it's sink or fucking swim, mate!' He was sitting forward and glowering at me, and the destructive energy coming from him seemed to pin me to my chair, before I freed myself as best I could by looking at my hands and lifting them slowly from the arms they seemed to be glued to. 'This feels so powerful to me – you have lost so much, Don,' I managed to say. The glowering anger in his eyes was fading now, as he whispered a faint 'yes'. I then suggested he could, if he wanted, sculpt another image of the medal and chain – one that might help him in some way, perhaps to see it from a different angle. Don did not take long to come up with a fresh sculpt, asking me to stand against the wall behind my chair, facing him with my arms up in a V shape. Images raced through my head – Jesus on the cross, an 'up yours' V sign and so on – but then when I saw the smile break on his face, I knew there was something more growthful at work here. 'It is back where it should be – around my neck,' he explained. We had been to his place of destruction – his valley of the shadow of death – his *nigredo* – the medieval alchemists' term for the deathly stage of the archetypal process which can move us towards a fuller, more individuated relationship to life and death (Mathers 2014). It was a moment where things seemed to begin to turn for him – a tipping point in response to the grip of a deathly complex, with archetypal and spiritual roots (he seemed to be a classic case of what Jung designated as the 'religious problem' at the base of our wrestle with finding our 'life-path'). Now, he seemed to be finding his way back on to this, and at last there was some hope, the spark of which would be kept alive with the container, the crucible (maybe the chalice?) of the faith he had left behind earlier in life. Over time, he found a church community which matched this new relationship to self and reality, as well as a partner who could see every reason to stay with him. Not an easy journey ahead, or a happy ending, but a good enough road ahead for Don.

On a 'technical' note, the way I approached this activity was to 'ladder' it. That is, I tried to pitch it at a level which worked for Don, as the client. Using the metaphor, if I had invited him to do the sculpting activity from the beginning, it might well have been too many steps up the ladder for him. So I put in the 'first rung' (the guided, body-based meditation), then the second (inviting him to allow an image to show), before the third (the sculpting activity). Instead of falling off the ladder towards insight and catharsis, this meant Don was able to get there in his own time, his own way, step by step.

To conclude

I hope this chapter has conveyed the power of creative approaches in working with spiritual themes, and the way these approaches can not only touch the depths of personal feelings and themes, but also open up questions of meaning, and being, at a more transpersonal and spiritual level. Used, carefully and judiciously, within therapeutic, pastoral or other spiritually related practices, supported by relevant training and supervision, they can open the door to the spiritual, and to the sublime, in its creative as well as destructive forms. These in turn can, with carefully structured activities which are responsive to the needs of the client, help the client with where they are, have been and may be heading. An opportunity for crisis of *being*, and crisis of *spirit*, can be used as a vehicle for growth.

Chapter 4

Contemplative Approaches to Training Spiritually Literate Counselors

R. Jane Williams

Introduction

In my decade of graduate-level teaching in training spiritually literate counselors, I have shifted my pedagogical emphasis from filling students with all the knowledge I can give them – every day, every lecture, every semester – to providing opportunities to learn and practice self-reflection, discernment, self-awareness, mindfulness, and silence, as tools to deeply challenge and help them integrate the knowledge they are gaining in the classroom. When they sit in a counseling room across from a client – Anton Boisen's 'living human document' (2005) – I want them to have the capacity to listen to what the client is saying to them and to their inner response and countertransference. Having practiced the contemplative arts of sitting with awareness, witnessing their inner responses, and letting go of thoughts and distractions, students are well prepared for the deep listening and non-anxious presence called for in many counseling sessions and situations.

Much like the reflexive groups that Gubi (2011c) recommends for training and support of clergy persons, contemplative practices used in the context of counselor training can be a personally and spiritually transformative experience. In our clinical counseling program, we have found that consistent use of contemplative practices (especially group spiritual direction, mindfulness meditation, use of metaphor, creative practices, varieties of prayer, walking meditation, poetry practice, pilgrimage, and retreat) in our supervision and peer spiritual direction groups increases students' capacity for deep inner listening to their own feelings, responses, and thoughts; to the client's feelings, responses, and thoughts; and to trusted others in supervision sessions or groups. Honing deep listening skills through reflective practices allows students to engage with, and integrate, counseling theory and knowledge with inner experiences of self and client, into meaningful counseling responses. Awarenesses and skills are developed by students in the context of having safe places, where silence and other contemplative practices are practiced, and students' questions and wonderings are honored. Students can take time to reflect among peers and instructors without needing to speedily produce a 'correct' answer. They can present their work for honest feedback, and try out ways of incorporating new insights in their next counseling encounter, in part due to the non-anxious instructor and peer presence, and support, that is established through group contemplative practices each week. Learning to trust and accept support from one's peers and instructors, as one shares personal and counseling case experiences, flows naturally from the emotional grounding and modulation lent by contemplative practice.

Contemplative pedagogy

Contemplative pedagogy, as employed in our counseling training program, uses contemplative practices to model and teach the core conditions of the counseling relationship: genuineness/authenticity/congruence, unconditional positive regard, and empathic understanding (Rogers 1986). Through the use of contemplative practices inside and outside of the classroom, students develop increased self-awareness, learn to notice, and nurture empathic connections, practice self-care, and increase their comfort with silence, pauses, and listening deeply. Students also begin to attend to how to integrate the counseling knowledge they have learned in more traditional academic classes into their work with clients in an authentic way.

Arthur Zajonc (2006a), one of the pioneers in contemplative pedagogy, characterizes traditional educational practice as *information in–information out* processes that focus on acquiring, organizing, and passing on information. Students who learn content are usually able to repeat it on tests or in discussions. However, for information to have meaning and to affect one's actions, a deeper connection to an organizing framework, or worldview, must be made. In other words, a student must engage with the material and evaluate its relevance to their existing framework of values, or review and re-evaluate their values, in light of the material.

One's worldview can become deeply ingrained as we habitually (and usually unconsciously) draw upon it to explain events and relationships. In perceiving someone's actions or words, we have a tendency to automatically interpret such actions or words in relation to our spiritual, or secular, value framework without considering alternative meanings, choices, or motivations. In today's culture, many of us compartmentalize our spiritual selves from our life in the so-called secular world, and fail to integrate, or even to acknowledge, spiritual values to ourselves, or others. Yet counseling core conditions are inherently spiritual – for example, valuing the other unconditionally, acting genuinely without protective artifice, seeking to understand and stand with the other in times of struggle. Contemplative pedagogy seeks to connect mind, body, and spirit through the non-sectarian practice of spiritual 'technologies' that are found in most religious and spiritual traditions, and seeks to bridge the disconnect between our spiritual and intellectual selves, promulgated by centuries of modernist thought. Contemplative practices encourage deep reflection and self-awareness, which can connect one's cognitive knowledge and interpersonal behavior with one's spiritual values. This holistic connection can transform one's practice of counseling from an hour of manualized problem-solving to a journey of discovery and healing that changes both counselor and client.

When contemplative pedagogy is used in secular higher educational institutions, practices are referred to as *secular* contemplative practices, and are used without religious references or language, and without intent to inculcate religious ideas. Even though our clinical counseling program is housed within a progressive Christian seminary, we do not use contemplative practices to influence our students to follow a particular spiritual path. We do, however, support and encourage students to come to know their own spiritual/religious traditions in greater depth, and to become spiritually literate, and knowledgeable, about major world religious traditions, through courses in world religions, biblical literature, and theological courses that include a variety of religious perspectives.

Educators using contemplative practices pedagogically are expected to have a well-grounded personal practice and be aware of the potential risks, and positive benefits, to students, of the particular practice. The authority of the position of instructor in a classroom makes it essential that one be aware that students may assume that we are encouraging them to follow our religious path. Although students should not be discouraged from exploring spiritual meaning in a practice, they should not be encouraged by instructors to follow a particular spiritual path. Barbezat and Bush (2014) encourage instructors to make clear to students what purpose the contemplative practices serve in their courses, and not use contemplative practice to promote a particular spiritual or religious path unless the course is clearly identified as providing instruction for the practice of a particular religion.

Contemplative practices in higher education include 'single-minded concentration, such as meditation; journal writing; mindful movement (yoga, t'ai chi, and dance); prayer; mindful reading; experiences in nature; artistic practices such as poetry, music, and spoken word; and forms of social activism in a context of mindfulness' (Edwards *et al.* 2011, p.1). All practices are intended to enhance students' awareness of their inner and outer experience, such that they can more deeply and personally engage with what they are learning (Barbezat and Bush 2014). In paying attention to their internal responses – the inner world of images and impressions – and their engagement with what they are learning, students come to see how content can affect their understanding of themselves and their behavior toward others, assist them in making, and seeing, meaning, and deepen their compassion for others. This often leads to profound understanding of how they might apply their learning to social action, in order to create change in their community and world (Barbezat and Bergman 2014).

Contemplative practices support multiple goals in the classroom and beyond, of which two are developing an ability to think critically about a topic and fostering an increase in compassion and empathy through growing awareness of the interconnectedness of all beings (Zajonc 2006b). As Tobin Hart (2004, p.28) observes, 'Long dormant in education, the natural capacity for contemplation balances and enriches the analytic. It has the potential to enhance performance, character and the depth of the student's experience.'

Compassion, empathy, and interconnectedness relate to spiritual values, despite being discussed in a secular context. Traditional higher education has focused on critical thinking, and on sharpening cognitive and analytical skills. The deepening of compassion, attention to values, and the concerns of the heart have, by and large, been left out of the purview of pedagogy, especially in higher education. Contemplative education, in its attention to self-awareness and interconnection, holds the promise that if we can learn to behold, and tolerate, the paradoxes and complexities we find within ourselves, we can better accept those paradoxes and complexities that exist in the world around us and consider with less reactivity and negativity the possibilities for peaceful co-existence. Freud (1894/2013) alerted us to the human tendency to be blinded to our inner dynamics through projection on to those outside of us. Contemplative practices teach us to slow down our primitive amygdala reactions, in order to manage our fear and anxiety, so we are able to explore our inner responses and make choices to see others through the lens of our interconnection to all beings. In a world that has the capacity to extinguish itself instantaneously with nuclear power, or more slowly with ever-increasing energy emissions, utilizing spiritual tools that awaken us holistically to the impact of our decisions (or non-decisions) on others (and ourselves) is work that nurtures a possibility that we might move toward a more just and peaceful world.

Training spiritually literate counselors

Currently in the MA in Clinical Counseling (MACC) program, one of our three primary instructors is a social worker and a trained spiritual director; another is a seminary-trained clergyperson and secularly trained psychologist, and a third is a secularly trained counselor with no formal spiritual training. Housed in an inclusive and progressive Christian seminary, the MACC program is holistic and seeks to integrate spiritual awareness with the skilled practice of counseling. Students' religious identifications include various Christian denominations and independent traditions, Muslim, Buddhist, Hindu, agnostic, or none. Our students take content-rich classes in counseling theory, diagnostics, and assessment, as well as a variety of theological disciplines. In these classes, pedagogy is fairly traditional. Students are exposed to religious concepts and current critical theological scholarship, through classes in world religions, New and Old Testament critical methods, and the history of religions in America. Consequently, counseling students become increasingly comfortable in an environment that speaks freely about religion and spirituality. Early in the first year, the norm is established that practicing and discussing one's spiritual path is welcomed, as long as there is a focus on understanding another, without the intent of conversion.

Among the many contemplative practices that we teach and use in our graduate program are silence (which begins every counseling class), mindfulness, sitting meditation, walking meditation, centering prayer, *Lectio Divina* (holy reading), poetry, reflective journaling, drumming, art, time in nature, yoga, Tai Chi, and mandala drawing. Students affirm to us that the contemplative practices they have learned help them quiet their minds and dissipate anxiety, as they begin to sit with clients. Such practices encourage, and grow, a deeper capacity for compassion, concentration, wise discernment, and insight, aiding students to accurately receive what others are communicating verbally and non-verbally.

While contemplative practices aid in emotional regulation, in strengthening relational skills in the classroom and therapy room, in exploration of personal meaning and values, and in clarifying one's call to vocation, they also serve as a means to grow appreciation for, and greater awareness of, the religious or spiritual tradition which the student brings with them. Some students find that in studying, and using, spiritual practices, they become more curious about their own tradition and are drawn to a deeper connection to it. Other students find that the regular practice of spiritual disciplines, such as silence and walking meditation, awaken in them a hunger to seek a deeper and different spiritual path. Contemplative pedagogy, with its attention to growing awareness of one's inner and spiritual self, tends to nurture a more balanced self – mind, body, spirit – regardless of religious or spiritual tradition.

We strive to develop in our students the capacity to be thoughtful, self-aware, spiritually inclusive, non-judgmental, open to where the client is, and able to accompany the client into difficult and dark areas of concern, without relying solely on problem-solving interventions. We identify our training process as a transformative one in the life of the clinician-in-training. Contemplative pedagogy, as we see it, is the use of contemplative, introspective practices in the classroom, with the intention of deepening students' self-awareness, insight, and deep engagement with counseling knowledge – and a catalyst for personal growth. Our intent is borne out by supervisors who frequently attest that our interns demonstrate a greater groundedness and personal and professional depth than students from other counseling programs. We have been asked several times, by supervisors, how we instill a more focused ability to sit with silence and track clients' thought processes than our supervisors are used to seeing in interns. MACC alumni report that counseling colleagues often inquire how they come to be so intuitively spot-on about client issues. Sitting with silence, practicing mindfulness, knowing and incorporating a variety of spiritual practices into one's life, is but one of the elements of the MACC program that creates a difference for our graduates.

First-year counseling students often assume that counseling training is about learning a catalog of techniques and content (e.g. pathology and diagnostics, interventions and theories) so they can solve their clients' problems (quickly). Learning to accompany clients on their journey, and using oneself as a relational tool (Aponte and Kissil 2016; Cooper-White 2006) is not on their radar. As research has shown, however, it is not specific therapeutic interventions, nor particular theoretical frameworks, that create client change, but the person of the therapist (Aponte and Kissil 2016; Strupp 2001; Strupp and Hadley 1979). Rogers' core conditions can be memorized cognitively, but embodying them in the person of the counselor and employing them in a therapeutic relationship requires another level of learning.

That deeper level of learning includes the ability to pay attention to, and witness, one's inner responses to the client. Our use of contemplative practices allows the counseling student to become aware of their inner responses, so that they can discern whether particular countertransferential reactions are a helpful resonance with a client's feelings (known as *totalist countertransference*) or with issues of one's own (known as *classical countertransference*) that need to be dealt with in one's own therapy (Cooper-White 2006).

In our module 'Introduction to Spiritual Formation', taken in the first semester, mindfulness practices are introduced and repeated in successive classes. Each spiritual formation class begins with breath work and silence, at first lasting two minutes, and then extended to 10–12 minutes over the course of the semester. Silence is always ended with a poem read aloud by the instructor that incorporates a theme of one of the spiritual practices (e.g. pilgrimage, contemplation, journaling) being discussed that day. Even students who disliked the silence at first eventually speak of how powerful such silence and mindfulness is in successfully transitioning from the 'outside world' to deep focus on the experience of the class.

One of the particularly Moravian spiritual practices used at our seminary is a variation of the *lebenslauf* tradition. The *lebenslauf* is a form of memoir, or life story, that Moravians have historically prepared before death, to share what they see as their legacy of life. At the seminary, *lebenslauf* is introduced in the first semester with the Dean and instructors sharing their *lebenslauf* orally with seminary freshmen. Such sharing sounds, and is, initially intimidating – even to instructors. However, the outcome is that hearing in others' stories something of what one may have experienced in one's own life builds a web of connection and community. Hearing one's instructors share life-journeys, including struggles and difficulties as well as joys and triumphs, helps students learn that it is safe to share oneself. During the first three weeks of the semester, students share their own *lebenslauf* in small groups. They then learn first-hand that what is shared can create warm connection, rather than judgment. In the MACC program, students have the opportunity to share a different aspect of their *lebenslauf* each year. Students express surprise at how their understanding of themselves changes each time they tell their story aloud, thus experiencing through repeated *lebenslauf* the subtle power of cognitive reframing.

Reflective assignments in all classes assess what knowledge a student has, and how that student is integrating that knowledge with self-understanding and growing in the ability to use it appropriately with clients. For example, when studying human development, students are assigned a paper that asks them to choose a faith/moral developmental theory, explore how that theory describes their development, and evaluate the accuracy and value (or not) of the theory in understanding their life experiences, and those of their clients.

Donald McCown (2016, p.31) speaks from a social constructivist perspective in noting that 'activities of teaching and learning mindfulness [are] an ongoing co-creation, involving and affecting all participants'. The roles of expert and novice are de-emphasized in our use of contemplative pedagogy. Learning is considered relational and MACC students' counselor identity discovered over time (rather than academically presented) through the mutuality of students and instructor. Modeling 'how to do counseling' is part of this, with the instructor working with students in a parallel process to what might happen in a counseling session.

For instance, in supervision class, a student might present a video of a case, and make a comment that she was frightened and uncomfortable, but did not know why, when she felt sexual interest coming from her client. The instructor might then ask the student to close her eyes and stay with the feeling of fear. Where in her body does she feel the fear? Is there an image or memory that comes as she lets herself feel the fear? A peer might observe that the student's breathing is shallow and faster than normal. Knowing how to use her breath to calm herself, the student might sit up a bit straighter, feet on the floor, begin to slow her breath and breathe more deeply. The instructor, or another student, might ask if she can direct her in-breath to the place of fear, and be aware of what is there. At the end of this time, the student might be asked to put the experience into words and share what she learned about herself. Did she notice a difference in her felt experience when she deepened her breath and sat up straighter? Was she aware that she occupied more space at that point, and appeared more confident and powerful? Peers might be invited by the student to share what they experienced of her process, sometimes noting synchronous feelings or counseling experiences. Peer-sharing is offered not out of a desire to correct her, but in a gesture of kinship and solidarity of experience. Such occurrences are probably not unlike what would occur in Gubi's (2011c) reflexive groups, only utilizing parish examples or cases.

McCown notes that those who use mindfulness-based instruction (another term for contemplative pedagogy) frequently hear from students that:

> [There is] power in being together...how strongly [they] value the sense of support of the class, how much easier they find it to practice with others and how 'close' they feel to people with whom they've spent precious little time. (2016, p.32)

Certainly that has been the experience in our MACC program.

Students report a felt difference between a classroom in which knowledge is tested and discussion is graded and a classroom in which knowledge learned is valued in the context of thoughtful application and experiential wisdom. Both are necessary. Contemplative settings allow appreciation of experience and internal knowing, alongside acquired knowledge. Because time is offered for students to pay attention to their internal responses to other persons, or to academic material presented, they sense the importance accorded to inner awareness and develop confidence to share with others what they perceive. Students experience the difference between accepting as 'truth' only what is pronounced by an expert, written in a textbook, or spoken in a lecture, versus trusting something when one has tested it internally and through putting it into practice in the world. Students begin to be less dazzled by the techniques and manuals of therapy, and become more interested in the person of the client, how to gain trust through a healing relationship, and how to respond genuinely, with, or without specific techniques, to the needs of the client.

Experiencing a non-anxious state in the classroom, and in supervision sessions, which teach and use breath work, silence, mindfulness meditation, and awareness without judgment, emboldens the student to do so with a client. In counseling practice, we know the 'other' through relational connection, rather than clinical, objective disconnection. Learning to create a calm, centered, mindful presence with a client, allows counselors to gain insight that does not come from intellectual apprehension or reasoning (Zajonc 2006a), but that is part of the subtle inter-subjective shared reality of the counseling container (Cooper-White 2006). When students learn how to acknowledge, and decrease, the normal anxiety that comes with being a novice in a counseling situation, they can calm themselves down sufficiently to focus on, and seek, intuitive, sensed understanding of the client, and allow themselves to more freely explore that connection with curiosity, rather than prescribed objective interventions.

As students progress in the MACC program, they eventually enter an 18-month period of practicum and internship. They remain in the same cohort from the beginning of practicum through graduation. Such long-term relationships build feelings of safety – safety which is made concrete through students' generation of, and periodic revision of, group expectations for how they will interact with and handle what is shared in the group. The group, or cohort, is essential for providing a safe place to process aloud one's inner perceptions and insights, and also to welcome and consider feedback on one's clinical work and case presentations.

We consider the supervision classroom (actually, any of our classrooms) to be sacred space, and we consider the classroom time we share as sacred time, set aside for the purpose of learning about ourselves and each other, so that we can offer healing relationships to others. Therefore, we create a classroom setting that exemplifies the importance of what we do.

Students and instructor sit together in a circle, or around a table, for easy eye contact. Each cohort circle time begins with a silent centering practice of at least ten minutes. Sometimes the practice is simply mindful breath work. Other times the practice is taken outdoors with walking mediation. The silence is broken with a gentle bell or chime, and is usually followed by the reading of a short poem embodying the theme for the day (e.g. listening to a client's pain, awakening to the gift of life). The instructor invites any responses, and then the cohort chooses an object from the altar (created by the instructor from candles and an ever-changing variety of objects from nature: leaves, stones, shells, plants, etc.) that calls to them in response to the query 'What has been your experience of the past week?' Exploring the details of the object, and connecting what they observe to their week, pulls them toward using metaphor.

The intentional use of poetry, song, and metaphor in describing one's experience has proven to expand students' capacity to step outside of their recent experiences (whether in the counseling office or in personal life) to mine them for rich insights, and to reframe their experiences resulting in new meanings. Using poetry is not just a lovely way to end the silence, but is also a means to move students to thinking in, and using, metaphors. Developing facility in using metaphorical images and language, as one reflects on assigned academic readings or one's experiences, results in deeper understanding of, and personal engagement with, how to put those learnings to use for healing with a client. Through use of metaphor and metaphorical language, students develop greater capacity for using what one knows creatively with a client – or for oneself – rather than blindly trusting and following a manualized or prescribed course of therapy.

Sensitivity to the inter-subjectivity present in the cohort circle comes with the repeated practice of silence and breath work, combined with debriefing, checking in with each other, and offering feedback to one another. Students become sensitized to their own inner process and hear others in the circle describe how they perceive each other. Relating inner, and outer, perceptions supports a student's willingness to check the accuracy of their perceptions with trusted members of their cohort (and eventually with clients). In learning to attend to inter-subjectivity as a source of wisdom, and a key to our relatedness (Cooper-White 2006), students also learn to hold lightly their assumptions about clients: to *offer* rather than *inform*, to *wonder about* rather than *assume*, to *suggest* rather than *direct*. In presenting cases for student and instructor feedback, students show progress throughout the internship year in moving from the expectation that they need to be the source of solutions for all client problems, to a humbler stance that honors the client's unique experiences, and identifies one's counseling role as that of a wise guide. The wise guide is one who journeys with a client, pointing out what may have been missed, or observing connections between events or behaviors, of which the client is consciously unaware. The wise guide lets the client choose a destination, and aids them in figuring out the path to get there. The wise counselor has a map, but does not choose the path.

An essential element of reflection in the MACC program is the tool we call *contemplative reflection* (formerly *theological reflection*). *Contemplative reflection* is a purposeful consideration of a counseling session through use of a contemplative practice and free association. *Theological reflection* has been used for many years within the clinical pastoral education (CPE) model as a way to train chaplaincy candidates in use of the *action–reflection–action* model of pastoral care. In the MACC program, we have adapted this model, including the verbatim and theological/contemplative reflection elements of it. *Action* in this model refers to a particular counseling situation involving the student in which something is troubling, puzzling, or particularly positive, and the counselor-in-training wants to understand it better. The *reflection* portion begins sometime after the session in question, and starts with remembering the session, especially any parts that were troubling, puzzling, or particularly positive. To reflect on this, the student enters a meditative state with eyes closed, using breath work to clear her mind and relax. When sufficiently relaxed and the mind is quiet, the student brings to mind the incident in question, or the particular part of the session. Next, the student free-associates to the memory, allowing whatever comes (an image, secular song or hymn, sacred text, sacred story, literary quote, etc.) to arise in their consciousness. Whatever arises first in one's consciousness is to be held on to as potentially offering clarification or an empathic resonance, relating to the session being considered. Students' tendency is frequently to question the validity of what comes to mind first as irrelevant, and to dismiss it. However, whatever arises in consciousness first needs to be one's focus for expanding one's understanding of the question. The next step in contemplative reflection is for the student to unfold whatever has arisen: if a song, look up the lyrics; if a sacred story, read it in its entirety; if a movie or story, remember it so that you know the whole story; if a quotation, find the context in which it was written or said. Almost invariably, when the image/hymn/story is seen in its entirety, there are surprises and insights that connect with, and enrich, one's understanding of the session in question, and deepen one's empathy for the client and oneself. For instance, during one student's contemplative reflection, the nursery rhyme 'Three Blind Mice' came to him. Looking up the lyrics led the student to let go of the humiliation and anger he felt toward a manipulative client who had recently relapsed into addiction, and instead to feel empathy for the client – and for himself. The student was able to see the client as someone who was *blindly* running with the crowd, not believing there would be consequences for 'one more drink' – consequences that resulted in incarceration and loss of the client's *tail/tale* (the client was a writer whose writing took a back seat to her addiction).

After analyzing how the image/song/story applies to the client's situation, students are asked to reflect on how the insights from the image/song/story apply to them personally. The student mentioned above realized that his angry response came from feeling *blind*-sided by his client's manipulation and relapse – and, rather than seeing the disease of addiction at work, he was caught in countertransferential feelings that the work he had done was 'just thrown in my face'. Applying the insights of the contemplative reflection to himself, the student was able to step back and see where he had been blind to the consequences of his need to see himself as a wise and successful therapist.

As Zajonc (2006b) writes, 'our way of knowing does, indeed, grow into a way of living' (p.1744). Because we want our counseling students to relate to clients with mindful, reflective, compassionate curiosity, instructors model mindful, reflective, compassionate curiosity in the classroom. As genuine, empathic, and reflective relationships are valued and established between instructor/supervisor and student, similar ways of being and knowing will be established with clients in a parallel process (Friedlander, Siegel and Brenock 1989).

Modeling respect, gentleness, intimacy, participation, insight, and vulnerability establishes an environment in which both instructor/supervisor and student/counselor-in-training are mutually engaged in a process of formation that results in the growth and transformation of both. Instead of the customary hierarchy of instructor as expert and students as novices, classroom relationships incarnate a mutual respect in which the instructor's authority of experience and advanced degrees are held lightly, and students' discoveries of relationships between learned knowledge and internal awarenesses are celebrated. Use of contemplative pedagogy, especially with students who will be working in the human services/counseling field, allows for the growth of an appropriate intimacy and trust in the classroom, between teacher and student, and among student peers. Relationships of trust encourage students to share their counseling work, mistakes and successes, while treating all shared experiences as fodder for learning and opportunities, to try it more skillfully next time. Contemplative practices create pools of reflective time in which our typical split-second responsiveness, or reactivity, is slowed enough to allow for mindful consideration of what one is perceiving and how one wants to respond. Contemplative practices highlight curiosity and wonder, and support a resolve to 'hold the truth lightly'. Post-modern thought recognizes that long-held truths are often more contextual than absolute (Doehring 2006). Instead of asking for objective right or wrong answers, the instructor in a contemplative classroom poses 'wonderings': questions that take material presented and 'wonder' about applications or experiences, in which students might imagine themselves. Guided imagery, metaphorical speech, role-play, or empty chair exercises deepen the students' experiences of these imagined scenarios. According to McCown (2016, p.35), 'The overall experience of being a participant in a mindfulness group produces a way of being in the continuously flowing and changing world, as opposed to a conceptual understanding of navigating a mapped and defined account of a world.' In learning, through mindfulness, how to notice, be aware of, and experience the present moment – to 'go with the flow' in class or in a client session – one places oneself within the present-moment experience rather than being separated from it, and learns 'how to get ourselves ready, so to speak, to go out to meet the events confronting us, rather than…working out how, instrumentally, to influence those events' (Shotter 2012, p.91). It would be hard to find a better approach as preparation for the unpredictability of the counseling setting.

Research into contemplative pedagogy

Research into contemplative pedagogy indicates that when contemplative practices are experienced within a group, the sense of emotional safety that develops may be due not only to higher-level emotional, and cognitive, observations, but to neurological processes at the cellular level.

Contemplative practice in a group allows a participant to visually observe other practitioners experiencing increasing relaxation, as may be seen in their relaxed body postures and softened facial expressions. Slowed respiration and calmer, quieter speech can be noted from auditory observation. These cues may signal to others in the room that there are no visible or auditory indications of danger so that they can trust the group enough to close their eyes and begin to focus inwardly. This intrapersonal experience of peace and safety cannot be fully accounted for by conscious analysis of observable cues. A sense of attunement ('feeling as one') to the group is described within some contemplative practice groups even when the group is new and they are strangers to each other. McCown (2016) notes that many meditators say that it is easier to go deeply into their contemplative practice when they are meditating in a group – even a group of strangers – than when they are practicing alone. Skeptics may question how one can sense a safe connection to others when no words are spoken, or acknowledgements made. Discoveries about the power of mirror neurons have helped to dispel skeptics' arguments that such experiences of group resonance are a fantasy.

Neurological studies continue to explore the existence and multiple roles of mirror neurons in the brain. Mirror neurons are specialized nerve cells whose purpose is to enable us to feel and experience others' body sensations and emotions, as though they are our own (Gallese 2009; Gallese and Goldman 1998). They work through mimicking within our brains what we observe another person doing or expressing. For instance, if we observe another person grimacing in pain, the mirror neurons in our brain signal our facial muscles to replicate that expression momentarily. We may not even realize this has occurred, so fleeting is our mirroring of the expression.

Nonetheless, it is enough to trigger in us the emotion that such an expression would signify if it originated with us. Mirror neurons activate the parts of our brain that mirror the activation in an observed person's brain, thus enabling us to resonate, or feel empathy, with that person, to experience a subtle indication of what they are feeling or experiencing. In one line of study, recent experiments have highlighted the possibility not only that visible expressions or actions can be mirrored/felt, but that the observing organism can also sense intentions and derive understanding of the behavior of others through the action of mirror neurons (Lacoboni *et al.* 2005). If this is true, it would still be important to validate one's suppositions of intentions or motives by checking them out with the other person!

Mirror neurons activate in two instances: when we act and when we observe someone else acting. This mechanism is automatic and, according to Gallese (2009, pp.520–521), allows 'a direct mapping between the visual description of a motor act and its execution'. Brain scans show that mirror neurons activate and allow us to resonate with sounds as well as visible actions. Because of the operation of these motor neurons in facilitating shared experience through perception and observation of the other, the separateness of experience that is assumed between one person and another is narrowed and an observer can have an internal 'mirrored' or felt experience of the other (Gallese 2009).

Combining our unfolding understanding of the function of mirror neurons with Porges' polyvagal theory (2011) may elucidate how the subtleties of facial expressions can mediate our sense of safety, or threat, in the presence of another. The vagus nerve is part of the parasympathetic nervous system and serves to relax us. This is in contrast to the sympathetic nervous system which stimulates us to fight or flight in the face of danger. The vagus nerve enervates the heart and also controls facial and neck muscles. Since mirror neurons supply data for the evaluation of safety, or threat, through the mirroring of facial expressions and sounds, someone's facial expression of anger, threat, or fear will be mirrored in our brains so that we feel the anger, threat, or fear as our own. Our amygdala responds to our fear and calls the sympathetic nervous system into automatic action – our muscles flood with glucose and our heart and respiration speed up to prepare us for fight or flight. If, however, we look around and see neutral expressions or smiles, our mirror neurons activate again, and our feeling of anger, fear, or threat begins to subside, and our parasympathetic nervous system is activated. The sympathetic nervous system steps back, the vagus nerve slows our heart and respiration, and softens our tensed facial muscles so that our expression can subtly convey the relaxation response that is slowly spreading through our body. 'And, for bonding, there is a release of the "love hormone" oxytocin, encouraging approach and embrace' (McCown 2016, p.33).

Just as McCown (2016) describes, our students' repeated practice of silence, contemplation, and mindfulness in every class establishes, through observation, a trust of the safe container. As their instructor, I observe the relaxation response being triggered in them almost immediately as they walk into the classroom and take their places in the circle. Sharing mindfulness practice repeatedly, and staying in the present moment with a cohort, builds the individual's capacity to stay with their experience, take in difficult feedback, and to tolerate, and use, the pain of personal struggle for growth. The increasing ease of activating the relaxation response generalizes to being with, and understanding, a client during counseling sessions. And it generalizes further when the counselor exhibits a non-anxious, relaxed posture and facial expression. The counselor's mirror neurons activate and begin to allow the client also to experience an increasing sense of safety and trust. The role of mirror neurons seems to lend credence to the counseling aphorism that anxiety in the room is contagious, and that a non-anxious presence is equally contagious.

Barbezat and Pingree (2012) note that building safety and attentional focus is not the only result of including contemplative practices in the classroom. A deepening understanding of the course content comes from students reflecting on it, and making it their own, through introspection. Students' deeper awareness of connection to others – in their cohort and with those they have never met – also comes with the practice of contemplation and mindfulness, via the action of mirror neurons. Through their attunement to the present moment, counselors-in-training can detach from their experience enough to notice what they are feeling and to notice how their feelings change in response to breath and awareness of them. Breath work becomes an essential, omnipresent tool to decrease anxiety, anger, and fear, and to bring oneself back to the present moment. Consequently, emotional regulation allows us to put aside intrusive thoughts and feelings, and refocus on the present moment, so that we can attend to the connection with the other in the room.

My colleagues agree that our supervision and peer group classes take on an almost mystical quality as students grow and mature in personal and spiritual awareness. A felt sense of the sacredness and preciousness of the time and space that we share as instructors and students grows as our work continues. In the course of studying with us, students who initially stumbled awkwardly as they tried to put into words their experience of spirituality come to comfortably use an inclusive language of spirituality that comes easily and naturally and is not tied to denomination or religion. And, most especially, students come to humbly acknowledge the sacred trust placed in us as counselors, by the clients who daily share their stories and struggles with us. The growth in humility, self-awareness, interpersonal connection, and compassion that we see in students as they graduate from our program is, in this author's opinion, a result of our belief in, and use of, contemplative pedagogy.

Chapter 5

The Use of Reflexive Practice Groups in Spiritual Development

Peter Madsen Gubi

Introduction

In this chapter, the use of reflexive practice groups in spiritual development and formation will be explored. A reflexive practice group is defined as 'a non-directive, closed group that aims to offer opportunities for reflection on interactions and processes in which reflexivity can take place at a psychological, relational and spiritual (theological) level' (Gubi 2011c, p.50). Rennie (1998, pp.2–3) defines reflexivity as:

> the ability to think about ourselves, to think about our thinking, to feel about our feelings, to treat ourselves as objects of our attention and to use what we find there as a point of departure in deciding what to do next.

Hertz (1997, pp.vii–xviii) describes reflexivity as 'an ongoing conversation about experience while simultaneously living in the moment', and Walton states that the types of questions that reflexive enquirers ask of themselves include:

- How does my personal history generate presuppositions that influence my approach to this topic?

- How does my gender/class/ethnicity/sexual identity/cultural location influence my understanding?

- Where do my allegiances lie and how do my commitments guide my approach to inquiry?

- What can my body and my emotional responses contribute to generating the knowledge I seek?

(Walton 2014, p.xvi)

In this chapter, the value of reflexive practice groups in counsellor training and their use in spiritual formation/development in the history of the Church will be elaborated. The psychological and theological benefits of reflexive practice groups will be explored, and the spiritual development and formation benefits examined. The chapter concludes with suggestions for how a reflexive practice group might run effectively today, using a focus for reflexivity.

The use of reflexive practice groups in counsellor training

Personal development groups are a form of reflexive practice group. Within counsellor training, the use of personal development groups is common in enabling core assumptions, beliefs, values and attitudes to be made visible to the person because of the group interaction. These colour our interactions and relationships with other people, and our perceptions and feelings about the world and the meaning of life (Johns 2012). Personal development groups can provide a space where assumptions, beliefs, values and attitudes can be fully revealed and tested in comparison with others' attitudes, through gaining responses and feedback from other people, and from seeing and feeling how behaviour, which is driven by our values, directly affects and is perceived by other members of our world. However, they do not always lead to positive outcomes (Williams and Irving 1996), and can sometimes be destructive (Lieberman 1981) and dysfunctional (Lennie 2000). Benson (1987) observes these 'negatives' as: feeling excluded or scapegoated; suffering the insensitivities, righteous, relevant or inappropriate anger and clumsiness of others; feeling unsafe and uncontained, over-dependent on or hostile to peers or group leaders; and feeling bored, frustrated, impotent or critical of self and/or others – all of which can occur for group participants at any time. Moon (2004) states that not all learners find reflexivity easy, and Robson and Robson (2009) argue that the need to feel 'safe' is important, and such groups do not always feel safe. However, Johns states that being in a personal development group can:

- [enable] experiencing interactions with other people in very concrete and immediate ways, which can reinforce effective interpersonal patterns, challenge unhelpful ones and allow for possible changes to be tested out;

- reduce loneliness and isolation connected with age and stage, life space or existential uncertainties by providing a supportive, bonded and, at times, loving connection with peers in shared, purposeful activity;

- provide opportunities to see and feel the consequences of our projections of others;

- offer, in other group members, a range of alternative models of being, behaving and communicating which may assist in us loosening or even changing some of our own constructs and strait-jackets in feeling, thinking and acting.

(Johns 2012, p.157)

Dryden, Horton and Mearns (1995) regard the personal development group as a vibrant context for identifying personal development needs. If an atmosphere of trust and spirit of encounter can be developed in a group, the members can help each other identify needs that might otherwise have been blind spots. Lennie (2007) states that the preferred size of a personal development group is between six and eight members, and environmental factors (e.g. the personality of the facilitator, the comfort of physical surroundings, the choice regarding fellow group members, the adherence to time boundaries) significantly affect the development of self-awareness, as do the opportunities for honest feedback available in the group. Lennie points out that the participants of personal development groups share relationships in other spheres which may affect how an individual communicates within the group, and whether they get to know others in a meaningful way or remain hidden within the group. Nonetheless, these groups provide a useful space for support, developing insight and improving relationality – all of which are important for underpinning the therapeutic encounter and developing the awareness and behaviours of the counsellor (Hall *et al.* 1999).

The use of reflexive practice groups in Christian church communities

Having encountered and facilitated personal development groups for a number of years, and found them to be not only potentially painful, but also, and more often, amazingly growth-promoting, I wondered if such groups could also be useful in spiritual development and formation. This led to some research (Gubi 2011c, 2016b, 2017). From searching through appropriate published literature, Rynsburger and Lamport (2008, p.116) state that one of the most endemic church trends in North America in recent times has been the use of small groups in adult spiritual formation, and that these are a response to a yearning for the sacred, and for community. Donahue and Gowler (2014, p.125) and Egli and Wang (2014) state that they are a place where 'belonging' can be had, and are a place in the spiritual journey that fills a void which is not met by family, formal church meetings or work interactions. Yet they are not a modern phenomenon (Bunton 2001). In my own faith tradition, long before any theoretical and psychological attempt to understand the value and function of personal development groups, the Moravian Church had some instinctive sense of the value of small reflexive practice groups, which Zinzendorf (the father of the renewed Moravian Church) called '*Banden*'. These were used to support the spiritual and interpersonal life of the Herrnhut community (also known as the *Herrnhutter Brethren* or *Brudergemeinde*). Each *Banden* was facilitated by a person who assumed primary responsibility for the pastoral care of the participants in the group. The quotation below is a description by Zinzendorf, dated to 1745:

> That we meet as Bands with each other, that we confess one to the other the state of the heart and diverse imperfections, is not done in order to consult with our brothers and sisters because we could not get along without the counsel of a brother or sister. Rather it is done that one may see the rightness of the heart. By that we learn to trust one another; by that no brother or sister thinks all the other that things are going well with some if they are really going poorly. Then no one can imagine that the brother or sister feels well when they are in pain. That's why you talk to each other, why you unburden your hearts, so that you can constantly rely on each other. (Cited in Freeman 1998, pp.259–261)

The following description by Christian David (one of the early Moravian missionaries) shows how these small reflexive practice groups were used:

> Initially there were among the brothers and sisters several who have a special trust in each other so that they began especially to form an association with the purpose (1) that they want to say to each other everything that they have on their heart and mind; (2) that they want to remind and encourage each other concerning everything they can see or think of each other and yet always to encourage one another to the good in everything; (3) that they want to come together once every week, in the evening, to hold conference or Bands with which they might get to know one another well within and without; (4) that they wish to give each other the freedom for heart, life, and journey, to test and express everything, and so love one another as their own life, to keep watch, pray, struggle and fight for one another, and to bear, spare one another, and help make life easier which is otherwise difficult, and therefore have the community which is proper to the Gospel. (Cited in Freeman 1998, pp.259–261)

Weinlick (2001, p.84) states that 'the unrestrained atmosphere of these congeniality groups served as both confessional and means of maintaining discipline and morale'. Podmore (1998, p.31) comments that Zinzendorf's *Banden* had the 'function of the confessional, and anticipated to some degree modern group therapy'. These groups were focused on the mutual confession of sin, were voluntary, and were focused on gaining unmediated grace through a direct encounter by the individual with the Holy Spirit that led to assurance (Watson 2010, p.4). They involved being mutually accountable, and being transparent with one another so each knew what was really going on in the depth of each other's lives in order to avoid self-deception and search their own hearts more fully – helping each other to see the true state of their own life with God more clearly (p.13). However, they could also be unstable. When 'no advantage appeared from these *Banden*, they were given up for a time and after a while renewed with a visible blessing' (Lewis 1962, p.56).

Having recently resurrected a research interest in these early Moravian *Banden*, Faull states that 'the Moravian method of self-scrutiny and pastoral care was gentle and probing, leading the religious subject to reveal insights about the self and soul, rather than forcing a confession' (2011, p.4). She argues that the Moravians saw this process as a 'walk with God and Jesus', and it was very much a process of self-care. 'Speaking, investigating, questioning, relating the experiences of the body and soul to a confidante, constitute a central moment in Moravian lives' (p.6). Helpers had to be confidantes of the highest order, with the ability to keep confidences and the discretion to avoid prying too deeply into the private emotions of individuals. He or she needed tact and a friendly trustworthy demeanour that invited people to open a window to the soul (p.7).

Bunton (2001) charts the history of such groups, suggesting that Zinzendorf's *Banden* were influenced by Lutheran cell groups during the radical reformation, and that their use was common in the Pietist movement. In the formation of Methodism, the Wesley brothers emulated the Moravian concept of 'Bands' but added 'outcomes' to their purpose in that they were expected to take people to another level of spiritual development, focusing on 'the right state of the Soul', and consisting of probing spiritual conversations.

So, reflexive practice groups have clearly existed in the Christian Church's history (Bunton 2001; Watson 2010), but it is difficult to find anything in current published literature about their value *today* in spiritual development or formation. This may be because of a fear of their non-directiveness and lack of control over the agenda, and levels of honesty that can engender uncertainty and silence, which people can be uncomfortable with, or which challenge the lack of authenticity that is prevalent in many church communities (Gubi 2011c). Other difficulties with relationship-centred approaches to small groups have been identified by Rynsburger and Lamport (2008, pp.116–126) as being: that spiritual growth in such groups can be problematic; that they promote 'feel good' spirituality rather than biblically based faith; that they assume that a simple loving and intimate community will promote spiritual growth, when what they promote and reflect are cultural values rather than spiritual values; that they discard a 'truth only model' and emphasise experience and relationships over biblical truths. Rynsburger and Lamport (2008, p.122) state that if scripture is simply viewed as a collection of individual faith journeys, which it is in relationship-centred small groups, it will hold less authority than a Bible that teaches timeless truths and doctrines. Rynsburger and Lamport (2008, 2009; Lamport and Rynsburger 2008) therefore argue for the centrality of scripture in small groups. Yet Heriot (2010) observes that small 'spiritual groups' are coming to define religion in North America. People join them to seek to heal and transform the self, and therefore the world. In them, the search for truth, healing and enlightenment is left up to the individual.

Within my own denomination, there is a renewed interest in some parts of the Moravian Church to reintroduce a form of 21st-century *Banden* (Graf 2012). Graf suggests that, should they be adopted again, the benefits would be that:

- The individual will develop his or her spiritual relationship with Christ.

- The individual will deepen fellowship with his or her peers.

- Active lay leadership will allow the minister more time for creative ministry and vision.

- The entire congregation will be reinvigorated by small groups of highly motivated Christians.

(Graf 2012, p.11)

Graf (2012) has pointed out that the characteristics of growing churches include an atmosphere of warmth, intimacy and authenticity in which members can rediscover the gift of spiritual discernment and also take risks, and suggests that heart-felt conversations in *Banden* (or reflexive practice groups) would help people to look across the aisle and see not a stranger in the pew – but Christ. However, there is a recognition that abuses of the system took place in the mission fields (Lloyd 1983), and Groves (2012) recognises that people can be reticent to talk about their walk with Christ even though they have not lost their spiritual vocabulary, and are deeply faithful and believing. Groves states, from her experience, that small groups can be dominated by people with relational or mental health difficulties, or strong egos. In a group context, some members can display 'super spirituality' which can alienate others, and there is always concern for gossip within small church communities. These are certainly things to be acutely mindful of. Yet should the value of such reflexive practice groups be dismissed because of potential difficulties, and might there be formational value in working through such difficulties as they arise?

The psychological benefits of reflexive practice groups for clergy and the wider church community

In my recent research into the use of reflexive practice groups to support clergy in the Church of England (Gubi 2016a; Gubi and Korris 2015), the benefits of reflexive practice groups were identified from the data as offering support, enabling clergy to feel less isolated, and enabling clergy to gain an insight into the way they think and into the impact on others of their way of being. Reflexive practice groups enabled clergy to respect difference better and to gain a better sense of self-care; they enabled clergy to engage in a better quality of pastoral encounter with others and to interact better with others in their ministry. Reflexive practice groups enabled clergy to grow as human beings, enabling trust and vulnerability to be experienced safely, and enabled clergy to negotiate boundaries better. They enabled clergy to feel listened to and valued, learn to listen to others better, learn from others, value one's own ministry more, have space to think and reflect, have permission to be oneself, and to gain the realisation that one is not alone in the struggles of ministry. They were a place to vent frustrations and express difficulties, and a place to reflect theologically and practically. There is no reason to suspect that these gains by clergy could not be had by other parts of the Christian community, if such groups were made available to a wider participation, aiding spiritual growth and formation.

The theological benefits of reflexive practice groups

Such a group is also an opportunity for reflexive (or autoethnographic) theology (Walton 2014) to develop. Reader (2008, p.73) refers to a concept of 'reflexive spirituality' in which 'what we learn about our own behaviour and processes of belief will itself inform what spirituality might become and directions in which it might develop'. This concept has been taken further by Wigg-Stevenson (2013, p.7) who states that 'rather than reflecting *on* Christian community or *on* Christian practice, Reflexive Theology highlights the aspects of doing theological reflection *in* Christian community and *as* Christian practice'. Wigg-Stevenson (2014) suggests that theological understanding emerges from both everyday experiencing and academic theology in a way that can embed, and embody, substantive contributions to theology and ethics. Taking this concept of reflexive theology beyond an ethnographic stance, in the context of a reflexive practice group (or community), where reflexivity is 'owned' and 'lived', it becomes an autoethnographic theological process (Walton 2014), in that theological wisdom and insight come from a tacit knowing that comes from 'within' in relation to what one experiences of the world, what one knows biblically and theologically, and where Christ is personally discerned. This is akin to what Zinzendorf described as a 'heart theology' (Freeman 1998), in which the *whole inner person* becomes the locus of religious knowing, rather than the rational mind:

> This inner person possesses all the senses which the outer person does, and by these senses in a way we might talk of today as 'intuition', or 'extrasensory perception', perceives the reality of Christ. The heart smells, sees, tastes, feels and hears… My heart tells me…it is thus to me. (Cited in Freeman 1998, pp.89–92)

This approach develops a tacit knowing, or discernment, of Christ, which can only come from a heightened sense of reflexivity, self-awareness and openness to how the 'Other' and Christ speak, and where one finds a sense of God in that. Insights of God are then tested against scripture and community to determine a shared validity. A sharing of that process within the safety and reception of a reflexive practice group enables a meaningful, relevant and transformational theology of the heart to be developed.

Davies (2013) seemingly echoes this kind of approach when he states that the key point of 'Transformation Theology' is that Christ is real, genuinely shares our time and space, and effects change through the Holy Spirit. If one is changed, then others are changed also, just as one is transformed by the change in others through Christ.

> Nothing is more personal than this kind of reorientation of life. But it is precisely where my life becomes most personal in this sense of undergoing real change, that I find myself positioned, in unity with others, before God the Triune Creator in Jesus Christ. At the point when I am most me, I find I am most him, or he is most in me, as I am in him… This is an inclusive, life-giving Trinitarian space. I know that others too are with me there, in whom he is and who also are in him, and I know too that it is the world – as it is transformed in him – that is the true source of change in me. (2013, p.18)

The essence of Transformation Theology, then, is to discern *where Christ is* in any given situation, and it is in the ordinary, as is constructed theologically, that Davies argues is 'the site of our potential encounter with Christ' (p.21). That which is transformative does the work of the word 'love' which Davies (2013) argues is fundamentally mysterious within the everyday (p.22).

The development of this kind of 'Transformative Theology', or 'Heart Theology', which can be facilitated in reflexive practice groups, raises the thorny question of 'authority'. However, Ravetz (2014) argues that *exousia* (authority) is present when we become aligned to the word (*logos*) within us. He encourages people to experience their own process of 'knowing' as a path to discovering their own authority:

> When we reflect on our thinking, we have created the thing we are knowing, and thus we are knower and known at the same time. This gives us confidence in our ability to know…and such clarity in our own inner authority liberates us from needing any outside authority. (2014, pp.15–16)

Ravetz terms this as 'logos-ology'. Although recognising the value of trusting in our own authority brought about by claiming one's own authority, such an approach is limited because it has the potential to be influenced by egocentric influences and motives that may not be 'of God' (e.g. selfhood). However, Ravetz (2014) claims that once we have found our true self through Christ (what he calls 'the seed-Word'), because we are all incarnational beings (i.e. the Divine lives within), we no longer need to hold on to the 'self': 'We would no longer be the centre of initiative in our own being; our identity would be that of the incarnate Logos' (p.106). Within a reflexive practice group, while honouring the logos-ology of each individual, the credibility, validity and authority of any theological insights that may arise may be tested against the experiencing, learning and wisdom of others in the group (i.e. within the authority of the community, providing their agenda is trustworthy), and, as in the Moravian context (Graf 2012), against the authority of scripture and tradition – which itself is open to interpretation and dialogue. There are also difficulties to 'logos-ology' when one thinks of situations when a person is convinced that they are called by God to ordination, for example, only for their sense of calling to not be upheld by the church community. One is left questioning the validity of their 'logos-ology' in such circumstances, or wondering if it is the church community that has got it wrong. Where, then, does authority lie? These (arguably) 'idiosyncratic' approaches to theology have resonances with Astley's (2013) notion of 'ordinary theology'. Astley (2013, p.1) defines ordinary theology as 'the theological beliefs and processes of believing that find expression in the God-talk of those believers who have received no scholarly theological education'.

Kelly (2014) refers to a 'theology of presence'. Although writing from within the context of pastoral supervision, Kelly refers to the development of the embodiment of reflection in practice, and then being able to risk responding and acting with *phronesis* (or practical wisdom). This leads to a theology that embraces risk as we face our vulnerable self. It risks staying with the 'mundane, even the boring, and being familiar with their patterns so that the treasure which points to possible transformation and glimpses of transcendence may be intuited and mined for' (p.47). This requires a reflexive, embodied self in order to create opportunities for personal and professional growth, characterised by tenderness, gentleness and grace, requiring us to love our neighbours as ourselves (Matthew 22.39) and to give forgiveness to self and others in a co-created safe space, secure in the knowledge that we are loved unconditionally by God. The embodied, reflexive self is the primary resource to facilitate the promotion of shared vulnerability and real possibilities of learning and transformation.

For some, these approaches to theology that reflexive practice groups have the potential to develop will be criticised as too idiosyncratic, not systematised enough, as potentially breaching Church teaching and tradition, or even heretical (Pattison 2007). However, reflexive practice groups provide the opportunity for developing the skills and attitudes required for meaningful experience, relationship and pastoral theological reflection and response.

The spiritual development and formation benefits of reflexive practice groups

In the context of ministerial training, Sims (2011) promotes the need for developing a 'capacity for reflection' in responding theologically to 'the complexity of ministry in an increasingly pluralistic world' (p.166). I would argue that this is true for all Christians, as we struggle to live out, and justify, our faith with others in an increasingly complex world. Sims draws on the works of Schön (1984) and Wolfe and

Kolb (1980), which place great importance on the 'tacit knowing' which, in the context of ministry and community, contributes to a *repertoire* of pastoral responses that spring from the unconscious, and enables a *knowing-in-action*. This *knowing-in-action* then leads to a *reflection-in-action*, then a *reflection-on-action* and then to a *reflection-for-action*. This, according to Schön (1984), is the process for the reflective practitioner. Sims (2011) argues that engaging in this process keeps vitality alive in ministry and faith, and prevents past mistakes from occurring (p.169). Developing these ideas within the context of training ordinands in the Uniting Church in Queensland, Australia, Sims (2011) states that he requires ordinands to write critically reflective reports on their ministry experiences, based on the following questions (summarised from Sims 2011, p.169):

- What did they do well?

- What was difficult?

- Were there logistical issues?

- What surprised them?

- How did the family receive their ministry?

- How did they sense that God was active in this situation?

- Would they do anything differently the next time?

Drawing on Wolfe and Kolb's (1980) learning cycle, but adding a theological perspective, Sims (2011) has developed the following further definition to the Four Stages of Adult Learning (see the non-italicised columns in Table 5.1). Sims (2011, pp.172–173) states that adding the theological perspective to the Four Stages of Adult Learning enables a theologically reflective ministry and faith in that:

- In *sensing the presence and action of God*, the person discerns where God is present and where God is acting. This requires humility and attentiveness.

- In *discerning God's purpose*, the person is required to stand back from the situation and reflect on what may be God's desires for the person(s) with whom they are ministering or encountering, as well as God's hopes for the way that they are ministering.

- In *integrating into one's theology*, questions of consistency with current practice of ministry or faith are asked. Holding the tensions within personal theology may be required.

- In *deciding to co-operate with God*, the person's personal theology may be revised, which leads to new implications for pastoral and ministerial practice.

All of these aspects inform the person's current and future faith development and practice. Sims (2011) states that if such reflective practice is engaged with, then learning can be deep, and different from much of the 'surface learning' that goes on in ordination training, Christian formation and journeying. He concludes that 'quality' ministry is more likely when theologically reflective practice is engaged in using his proposed theological lens of 'sensing the presence and action of God, discerning God's purpose, integrating into one's theology, and deciding to co-operate with God' (p.175).

Table 5.1: Adding reflexivity to Sims (2011) Further Definition to the Four Stages of Adult Learning

Learning Strategy	Learning Environment	Primary Mode	*Reflexive Perspective*	Theological Perspective
Concrete Experience	Emphasising Personal Experiences	Feeling or Getting Involved	*Growing awareness of how I am feeling*	Sensing the Presence and Action of God
Reflective Observation	Understanding Concepts	Watching	*Awareness of what this is tapping into for me*	Discerning God's Purpose
Abstract Conceptualisation	Preferred Logical Thinking	Creating Ideas	*Making sense of how I am feeling and responding*	Integrating into One's Theology
Active Experimentation	Applying Knowledge and Skills	Making Decisions and Doing	*Trying out a different way of being*	Deciding to Co-operate with God

(from Gubi 2016b)

Sims' (2011) notion of theological reflective practice has much to commend it, but to make it *'spiritually reflexive practice'* I would suggest the addition of another column focused on *reflexivity*: 'What am I noticing about myself in relation to the other, and how might I "be" different?' (see the italicised column in Table 5.1). This further level of awareness required of reflexivity enables a deepening of the awareness of the part (and the past) that the person brings to the encounter, or to the experience, that they are faced with. This, in addition to the other areas of attention identified by Sims (2011), arguably provides a more reflexive response, which enhances self-awareness and deepens insight, enabling a better pastoral and theological response, in keeping with the development of reflexive theology and reflexive practice.

Things that may hinder the reflexive practice group

My research (Gubi 2016b) revealed that the hindrance factors to reflexive practice groups were:

- Participants were unable to prioritise and commit to the time.

- It was scary for participants to open up to their vulnerability with others.

- Sometimes the needs of some of the participants were too big, and could sabotage the group.

- Dual relationships with other group participants could cause complexity and hinder sharing.

- Prayer was not helpful where it was used to spiritualise away or 'make better'.

- Being sent by someone in authority meant that the experience was not voluntary.

- The open agenda and style of facilitation does not suit some people.

- Sometimes there are struggles with expectations because the reflexive practice group is culturally different from other groups found in church community settings (i.e. What is this group about? What is expected of me?).

- Geographically, the distance of the reflexive practice group was prohibitive for some, although having to travel provided another reflective space for others.

Other hindering factors expressed in the data included external factors that were 'around' for participants (e.g. significant personal difficulties), and the difficulties with dual boundaries.

Although the concerns and experiences expressed in the data are important things to be mindful of, and echo, to some extent, Miles and Proeschold-Bell's (2013) research, the overwhelming evidence from the research (e.g. Gubi 2016a; Gubi and Korris 2015; Barrett 2010; Travis 2008) is that reflexive practice groups are beneficial for psychological and spiritual well-being and growth (formation).

How reflexive practice groups might look in practice

So, as a means of formulating practice, the following foci for reflexivity are advocated (see Figure 5.1). These foci for reflexivity enable a fairly systematic yet fluid approach for the development of reflexivity within the reflexive practice group context, and include the psychological and the spiritual/theological. Recommendations for instigating reflexive practice groups are:

- The reflexive practice group should not be structured in its content (i.e. it is non-directive, but focused on psychological and spiritual process, holding the foci for reflection in Figure 5.1 with attention). The content emerges from what is 'around' for the group participants.

- Reflexive practice groups should consist of between six and ten participants who negotiate an agreement (covenant or contract) consisting of confidentiality and practicalities (time, place, frequency, cost).

- The reflexive practice group should meet weekly in theological colleges/seminaries (preferably), and monthly in dioceses or church communities, for at least one and a half hours (preferably two hours).

- The reflexive practice group should be facilitated by an external facilitator (preferably a counsellor/psychotherapy-trained and not on the staff of the same theological college/seminary as the participants or likely to have dual relationships with participants) who is trained in group facilitation and group process, and who is able to facilitate at a spiritual- and psychological-process level.

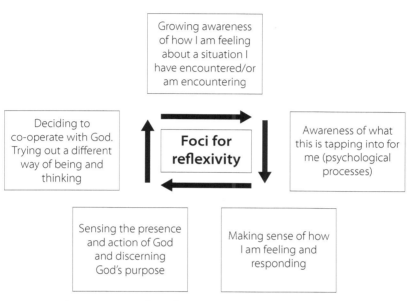

Figure 5.1 Foci for reflexivity in reflexive practice groups

- The facilitator keeps the group focused on the internal reflexivity task, and the sharing within the group of that, embodying and exemplifying a quality of servanthood, service and hospitality. The time is not to be divided equally between participants, nor does everyone have to speak. However, a good facilitator will 'notice' and 'invite' non-contributors as appropriate.

- Participants, too, will be encouraged to listen deeply, share appropriately and facilitate each other with the foci for reflexivity in mind.

- Having two facilitators for each group has its own (arguably useful) dynamic; given the limited financial resources in many communities, however, having two facilitators is not necessary.

- Facilitators mindfully hold awareness of the aspects that may limit a group and do what they can to overcome them where possible.

- Because there is always the potential for the process to become unhelpful, facilitators will need to be in supervision.

- Facilitators will also need to be able to facilitate fluidly in ways that move relatively easily between the spiritual (theological) and the psychological.

Conclusion

As counselling/psychotherapy and spiritual accompaniment/direction come more into dialogue and learn from each other rather than focusing on their differences, methods of training and development, such as the reflexive practice group, can aid in both the psychological and the spiritual development of those with whom we journey. However, used in either a psychological or spiritual context, the reflexive practice group is impoverished when either the spiritual or the psychological is excluded. The foci for reflexivity, which this chapter advocates, enable a more holistic development to take place, which fosters spiritual formation and psychological well-being.

Chapter 6

Grieving for Myself

The Silence and Spirituality of Personal Loss

Ruth Bridges

Introduction

This chapter began 25 years ago in the intensive care unit of a small general hospital in the North West of England. I was 23, recovering from an emergency hysterectomy as a complication of childbirth, and I was in shock. I was also learning, although I did not realise it at the time, how to listen to the pain, loss and grief of others. Illness presents a uniquely intimate experience of loss, and facing death through illness is a uniquely intimate experience of grief. This chapter considers those for whom a diagnosis of significant or life-threatening illness has provoked a sharp realisation of their mortality and who, thereafter, live with an acutely conscious awareness of their dying. I include, with permission, reflections from a research discussion (in italics) considering the challenges of living with illness offered by a small group of colleagues who work, therapeutically, within this realm. I am acutely aware that we represent a particular time and place, clearly 'historically and socially situated in ways that [were] given… rather than chosen by us' (Carel 2008, p.94) but, together, we offer over 50 years' experience, and represent many voices.

This is a desperately important and essentially spiritual realm that, for too long, I believe, has been somewhat silent within both counselling and pastoral care. I rather suspect, however, that I would not feel so strongly were it not for my own near-death experience. For this, and for the existential crisis it prompted, I am profoundly thankful. The ten years I spent offering counselling/therapeutic accompaniment within cancer care acted as a vivid reminder (if I needed one) that our spiritual/existential being and process is held very concretely within our physical form – 'our existence…forever shadowed by the knowledge that we will grow, blossom, and, inevitably, diminish and die' (Yalom 2008, p.1). How, therefore, do we live while holding a true acknowledgment of our transience? And how, as those striving to offer emotional and spiritual care, might we enable such knowing to be experienced by our clients for what it is, within all its grief and pain: *You are waiting…and it's purgatory.*

Although the fields of spiritual and pastoral care overflow with literature considering the process and experience of the death of others, far fewer texts consider grief from the perspective of our own dying. 'Dying is at once intensely threatening and intensely personal,' offer Sullivan and Mason (2006, p.122); our physicality is particular to us, with its own texture, form and language. The uniqueness and loneliness of experiences of physical helplessness may, therefore, greatly amplify our sense of being adrift in the universe.

I have become acutely aware of my body while writing this chapter, lost at times within some difficult and demanding places. In the midst of this, I have wondered, again, of the impact of my own loss and pain on my capacity to hear the losses and pains of those I accompany. Do we, at times, delude ourselves? Do our own vulnerabilities truly open us to hear the vulnerabilities of others, or do they simply heighten our own sense of existential isolation? Is it possible, perhaps, that they might do both? However experienced, compassionate or grounded we might be, as Roy (2005, p.235) challenges, 'from what height or depth could one possibly *presume* to speak? Let us, therefore, approach with great humility those conversations we are yet to have for ourselves but might still be privileged enough to witness in another.' 'A house can only fall down once and then the dust settles,' offers Coutts (2015, p.34). Whatever form the 'fall' and any subsequent settling might take, my hope, as counsellor and spiritual accompanier, is to bear faithful, loving and empathic witness to such without collapsing into my own 'ineptness' (Glaser and Strauss 1965, p.5).

A uniquely intimate loss

Surely we should all be 'dwarfed and humbled by the largeness of our trajectory toward ageing, decline, and eventual death', suggests

Pizer (2009, p.80). Are we, though, so overwhelmed with stories of death that we become habituated? The immediate and intimate reality of our own life, or of those closest to us, assuming a surreal nature. The 'diet of horrors' (Sontag 2003, p.95) we are fed prompting a certain detachment perhaps. Have we become so familiar with seeing suffering through a screen, or via a newspaper, that when it draws near we barely recognise it as the same thing? Perhaps, as may be more likely, we do not dare recognise it as the same thing, for to do so means we must accept we are fragile beings and that life holds itself precariously, always.

The boundaries between capacity and incapacity, independence and dependence, health and illness are easily breached and can feel achingly bleak. We may find very 'little recognition of, or support for, the work of living and dying over time' (Nicholson *et al.* 2012, p.1426). Without warning and often at great speed, it is into a state of 'persistent liminality' that we are thrown, I believe, when diagnosed with a significant illness. It is here, however, that we must learn to navigate ourselves if we are to continue to engage with life in a way that is sufficiently consistent with our sense of self so as not to render us entirely lost. 'Reading about death and illness is nothing like receiving a dire medical prognosis…the tightening chest, the cold panic washing over you; these are so visceral, so traumatic, so real,' reflects Carel (2008, p.117). This, as O'Mahony (2016) proposes, is not something we can simply imagine ourselves into. 'It is all too easy, from the position of robust observer, to envision as intolerable a life of restriction and pain but we would do well to accept that the instinct to live is…powerful, and in our health and vigour we underestimate it' (p.187). Priorities and perspectives change.

I suspect anyone who has experienced a moment of diagnosis can remember the sensation of that moment with the sharp accuracy of all seminal events, even if the details themselves have blurred over time.

> He was kind but direct; the news was not good, I had an adenoid cystic carcinoma in my sinus and it was malignant… I don't recall being very shocked or afraid, simply that I had entered a void over which I had no control. (Finlay 2013, p.64)

Whether in a surgery or at home, finding the lump or acknowledging the pain introduces into our narrative a very distinct 'before' and 'after'. Coutts (2015) expresses this with the heavy authority that can only come from having lived it. 'The news,' she reflects, 'falls neatly between one moment and another. You would not think there was a gap for such a thing' (p.2). Indeed, part of our confusion is often the apparent seamlessness of everything around us. As we reel from the shock of diagnosis, the world continues without pause. And yet, within this same world, there are numerous moments, just like this, arriving unannounced – changing lives. However we may grow into the loss and pain of our particular prognosis, that moment marks the turning. Life will not be the same again. *There's a new awareness, a new awareness of frailty and vulnerability…and that life can turn on a sixpence…and if it's got you once it can get you again.'* 'We know,' reflects Dowling Singh (1998), 'that the initial announcement of one's prognosis…is almost inevitably a moment of perceived and profound tragedy. It is a moment of deep and violent psychic pain and incredulity' (p.88). In many of our writings about grief we appear to have rather calmly overlooked the violence and tragedy of 'one's prognosis'. In so doing, we have, I believe, denied ourselves the right and the responsibility to feel the level of compassion for ourselves that we can be so willing to offer to others. Might we ever redress this balance, I wonder?

Clients have often replayed for me their particular moments of discovery and have relived, often within immense pain, the profound shock they felt on realising that 'the prized integrity of [their] body had been intruded on' (Murphy 2013, p.72). It is so important for us to be congruently and compassionately present with our clients as they take us back to those moments, where past, present and future coalesce – the rest of life, suddenly and simultaneously, feeling 'meaningless and extraordinarily meaningful' (Frommer 2005, p.484). These can be deeply disorienting experiences. A face in the mirror no longer quite familiar, a body shape that does not belong. Medication on the kitchen worktop. Foods no longer enjoyed or no longer 'allowed'. Hair on the pillow *'identifies you as a cancer patient. Once it's in your narrative you can't remove it can you?'* Clothes too large or too small. Sex impossible. *'At what point do you tell your date [that you can't have children]? Do you get it over and done with and let them walk off then and there?'* Great loss. Profound and personal. Life being taken away, piece by piece.

It is rare, however, for clients to linger long over some of these losses, as if not legitimate somehow. Often it is not until I reflect on their meaning (offering permission maybe) that tears and anger may surface. Here, any 'illusions…of perpetual health and immortal immunity' have been well and truly 'punctured' (Pizer 2009, p.80). *'I think that's one of the biggest losses...the loss of complacency.' 'It never goes away...that altered normal.'* For me, this loss cannot be stated enough. Loss of body parts, of fertility, sexual function, digestive capacity, bladder or bowel control. Deeply difficult to discuss and desperately hard to bear. Hidden and silent, yet loud within us.

Some clients may fiercely guard their physical boundaries through this time, whereas others may need, and want, to talk freely and openly about their bodies, as if a threshold has been crossed. *'You do find patients become more ready to expose their bodies...they are more ready to share...it's almost like, "Well, everybody else has had a look at me and examined the intimate parts of my body, why don't you?"' 'That wanting, somehow, you to see the scars...almost like they've shown you all the emotional scars but you have to see the physical ones.'*

Physical scarring, of course, can assume a presence and a prominence that is impossible to disguise – however much our clients may wish to do so. As Henry (2011) reflects, 'disfigurement influences the way someone lives their life' (p.280), and this living, surely, is at every level, from the most concretely mundane to the most esoteric.

Clients may move from a reassuringly reliable independence, to a disturbing and unpredictable dependence. And, unlike infants, as Frank (1995) asserts, 'when adult bodies lose control, they are expected to attempt to regain it if possible, and if not then at least to conceal the loss as effectively as possible' (p.31). *'The stuff people have to deal with, with this, is just massive...just massive.'* Moments of bodily exposure, of catheters and nasogastric tubes, blood tests and stool samples. We may need to adjust to mastectomy, tracheostomy, amputation. *'That sense of identity when it comes to appearance...what they think people see...when that emotional scar feels so raw.'* And, as Henry (2011) also offers, alongside our personal battle of adjustment and re-adjustment comes the shame that 'disfigurement is regularly aligned with having a damaged personality' (p.276). *'It's the emotional pain, the emotional ugliness of what I'm really feeling inside here.'* Are we swept, therefore, into a profound and pervasive silence? Embarrassed into concealing our losses; learning the language of illness and, more disturbingly perhaps, what culture and society may demand of us through it?

Silence does not, and should not, infer there is no loss, but that there are no words or, perhaps, that 'to lay [that loss] bare...feels like a violation' (Kerr 2013, p.146). As a counsellor or spiritual accompanier within this realm, I wonder how many times I might have missed the subtle, unvoiced signs that profound existential struggle was being contained rather than expressed. These can be heavily veiled and silent spaces and yet, paradoxically, desperately full and screaming. Everything shifts, and yet it continues to amaze me how quickly we are able to adjust to this new landscape – how our narrative stretches, however agonizingly, to accommodate our changed reality. This stretching, however, can feel unnervingly surreal and, whether it is induced by fear or medication, clients may be left feeling they are 'drowning in a world adrift somewhere between logic and reason' (Mayne 2006, p.245). A passionate advocate of the significance of attuning to the presences of our clients, I believe we need to become acutely aware of changes within process and relationship that may indicate something is happening, something in whose presence we need, as therapists and accompaniers, to remain steady and unafraid.

'Cast out of the Eden of our mindlessness' (Moore 2010, p.77), we turn, perhaps, to different languages and ways of being. Life can assume a far more real and raw form. Frightening it may be, but clients may experience living in a way they have not experienced before. They may glimpse, even, something of the intoxication described by Broyard (1992). Values, beliefs and hopes can change radically. 'Receiving health news which states that a condition is inoperable or incurable presents a crisis situation' (Tann 2013, p.14). This is a place of trauma – a trauma that continues to be lived. I have worked with numbers of clients through the years who have grappled with both the gifts and the agonies of such traumas. They are acutely demanding and essentially spiritual, whatever language is used. This can be deeply disturbing for those who stand as witness to such processes, hoping their partner, parent or child will spring back into a familiar and predictable shape once the immediate crisis has passed. They do not. Indeed, they might not want to be back at all. 'At times I wished…that my heart had failed totally and comprehensively' (Andrews 2013, p.46).

As listeners, opening ourselves to hear such declarations, with understanding and without fear, is so very necessary if we are to offer the accompaniment demanded of us at the depth required. And, all the time, *'everybody had their expectations – "No you're a fighter, you've done it before, you can do it again." They found all those expectations really, really difficult. They just wanted to run away and not fight.'* I have often witnessed with clients the sense of turbulence that accompanies diagnosis and treatment, the sense of life becoming something else entirely – relationships being strained to breaking point, priorities changing, a level of awakening bursting dramatically into consciousness. They are moving at a different speed to those around them, it seems. Deeply confusing, and, all the while, 'the future curls in on itself and at once becomes both exposed and radically curtailed. It has a clear endpoint' (Carel 2008, p.123).

Years pass and I enter middle age realising, with some shame, the naivetés I have held. We have all 'lost the ability to accept illness, aging, and death as natural parts of life', claims Toombs (2004), holding, perhaps more than we dare acknowledge, 'unrealistic expectations about the power of medicine to…keep us alive' (p.194). How do our own illness narratives permeate the spaces we share with our clients? If we are afraid, how might we hear fear in our clients? If we hold hope of existential permanence, do we truly have the capacity to hear another's dread of 'vanishing away' (Adelbratt and Strang 2000, p.503)?

Nicholson *et al.* (2012) highlight the importance of finding 'anchor' points within 'imbalance'. These are surely of fundamental importance within the navigation of illness, pain and dying. These anchor points might be internal or external. They might encompass religious or spiritual practices; they might take the form of an object, place or relationship. 'Facing death through illness can sometimes push you to the very edge of your understanding and emotional strength,' reflects Moore (2010, p.86). A regularly predictable therapeutic space can offer a deeply important foothold when we feel close to those edges, and all else seems chaotic; 'all our accepted priorities…thrown into disarray' (Finlay 2013, p.63). Ours might be the only relationship within which truth can be spoken, unvarnished, where ideations of self-harm or suicide can be expressed without fear of ramifications. It is critical, then, surely, that we strive to hold an honest awareness of aspects of our own grief, pain and loss. Important too that we do not slip into assumptions and expectations regarding the lives and experiences of our clients. We may, at times, witness what O'Mahony (2016) describes as 'a remarkable indifference, a lack of curiosity'. He goes on to suggest that 'this is not an unusual reaction to serious illness', suspecting 'it is some form of primitive reflex that protects our personality from disintegrating in times of crisis' (p.68). For those of us who are striving to work within the realm of spiritual accompaniment and counselling, do we, and can we, offer a safe enough space within which our clients might express their indifference or feel their disintegration, if it threatens? Or do we hover fearfully on the threshold, persuading ourselves that appropriately ethical practice demands a level of distance so that our clients do not become 'dependent' upon us? This is deeply, and inevitably, intimate work, but the very nature of these losses means there is an essential aloneness here. An aloneness and a grief within which we cannot be fully accompanied, however courageous our therapist or accompanier, and however closely we may sometimes be held.

On grief and grieving

'Many dying people pause at the point of departure,' states Hockley (2015, p.170), but how is it when the pause is not counted in hours or minutes, but in weeks and months? How do we live this? How do we encounter our dying in a way that honours our living? How might those around us hinder or help us as we strive to do so? *'The pressure on them to get it right; they've been given this time so they can say their "goodbyes" and they can get it perfect...and...what's that?'* As previously stated, much of our literature regarding grief centres on the experience of loss from the perspective of the observer, rather than from the experience of grief when faced with the loss of ourselves. 'Grief is a powerful experience that cracks us open and leaves us immensely vulnerable,' reflects Granek (2014, p.61), so how might this grief feel when the life we mourn is our own? How do we become the griever and, simultaneously, the one for whom we grieve? Inextricably bound. As someone who offers emotional and spiritual care, my role, I believe, must be to hear both. To bear sensitive witness to the part(s) in mourning and the part(s) that die(s). Holding the tension, the ebb and the flow, the contradictions.

Grieving and dying simultaneously offers, and demands, a profound awakening; 'everything is evolving into something other than what it was' (Smith 2015, p.133). Experiencing both within us may take us to places of great pain and great beauty, may deepen and heighten the experience of being alive and may terrify us. *'It's just a matter of time...it might be years...but in those first few weeks and months I think that is an enormous chasm that people drop into that they just can't see a way out of.'* The way clients comprehend such loss is surely of significance here. As Dowling Singh suggests (1998), loss, diagnosis, pain, dying may be perceived, variously, as 'punishment, long feared as retribution for self-judged wrongdoings...as life's statement of their lack of unique value in the universe…as harsh fate…a challenge to meet with courage…or one more entry in a long list of bitter disappointments' (p.97). This existential process needs somewhere to be voiced, I believe, or we may feel we implode with it. Grieving for ourselves, with integrity, is surely an immense undertaking – one that demands a level of focus that might appear self-indulgent, even obsessive, to those around us. *'You find people completely reassessing where they were and thinking – "Well, do you know what…if I'm on a different time frame now I'm just going to have a blast and it'll be two fingers to anybody who doesn't like it!"'* Conversations may be 'closed down' by well-meaning friends and family who fear for our psychological safety, or who cannot bear the agony of it themselves – '[t]he collapse into gut-wrenching pain, the emotional anguish, the mental numbing' (Heath 2014, p.296). Clients may disappear into depression or explode into action, both of which the same well-intentioned friends or family members may try to cheer or persuade them out of. Lost in a world as yet unknown, while living within the ordinary reality of the everyday requires a huge amount of physical, emotional and spiritual energy, the impact of which should not be underestimated. 'There is something here I did not know before,' offers Coutts (2015) with desperate poignancy. 'I thought that there were limits to the absorption of pain. I thought that it was finite. I thought that it would stop' (p.63). Whether through the gradual decline of the aging process or the rapid and perhaps more existentiality shocking trajectory into loss through invasive surgery, treatment or illness, our sense of self is changed. I might have to develop a very different image of myself and I might not want to. I did not grieve following my hysterectomy, for I had no idea how to do so. Also, importantly, I had no idea I was 'allowed' to do so. Having survived this 'particularly potent nudge into consciousness' (Moore2010, p.77), I was deeply thankful to be alive and turned any energy I had outwards.

As time passed, however, I often found myself weeping profusely when I was on my own, not quite knowing why. I prayed to a God I was no longer sure I believed in but was too terrified to let go of. I pleaded for understanding, and for some release from the darkness. My body and my mind powerfully 'in charge' (Kerr 2013, p.154), I felt completely helpless, afraid and utterly 'alone with my existential thoughts' (Axelsson *et al.* 2012, p.2156). Throughout this time my daughter continued to grow, mercifully unaware (as far as that was possible) that her mother was unravelling and had absolutely no idea what to do about it. Staring death in the face had indeed provoked something that I battled to negotiate on my own. However much I pleaded for the pain to be taken from me, I absolutely believe, in retrospect, that my 'depression' was 'an appropriate response' (Moore 2010, p.76) to what I had gone through. Attention that I had received in the weeks after my surgery had, understandably, been on presenting physical symptoms and bodily needs; similarly, for the majority my clients. *'It can be difficult for clients to constantly be told, "You'll be OK" and "Well, you've beaten cancer so we should be on the up."'* There is a danger, I believe that, even if our bodies heal, our souls and spirits may remain very much damaged.

'Dying…is lonely – the loneliest event of life. Dying not only separates you from others, but also exposes you to a second, even more frightening form of loneliness: separation from the world itself' (Yalom 2008, p.119). What of our spirituality here? Does a sense of God, faith, spirit, offer us a foothold when the ground begins to fall away, or does that feel as threatened as everything else in the wake of such crisis? Are we 'faced with the withdrawal of God' (De La Mare 2013, p.27) or is our diagnosis 'proof' that God never existed in the first place? Are we being tested? Will we be saved? 'One would think, intuitively,' asserts O'Mahony (2016), 'that death and dying would be less terrifying for those with a strong religious faith', and yet he does 'not believe that is so' (p.231). As a teenager, I belonged to a faith community – a community that fervently believed in the will of God experienced as much through suffering as through joy. Seriously ill members were often profoundly hurt and frightened by the claim that they did not have enough faith to be healed. The will of God was strongly cited, and debate was not encouraged. We did not dare to question a God to whom we were supposed to entrust our individual and collective futures. Essentially, 'tied up with totems and symbols and arguments' (Rohr 2003, p.94), the community largely avoided true engagement with, and within, matters that might have shaken some of their sincerely held beliefs or, perhaps, have threatened the delicate infrastructure of the organisation itself. Many were left in great pain.

Conversely, however, God and our faith community may offer incredible comfort and peace. Being held is something my clients have often referred to, and I know unequivocally that this holding was, for many of them, spiritually experienced. In a more tangible sense, the reading of scriptures, prayers, chants, sacred texts or the offering of music may contribute to an environment of well-being, easing the transition, perhaps, between this world and the next. We must be wary of intent here, however, that our own desire for comfort does not take precedence over the needs and wishes of the one who is dying. As listeners to grief and pain, we need, I believe, to maintain acute spiritual sensitivity. Through listening, with openness and care, for those moments within which their God (however envisaged) might be being questioned, challenged and doubted, as well as trusted, loved and worshipped, we can offer clients the opportunity to potentially begin to discover the depth or, perhaps, demise of their faith – maybe both. Clients may experience moments of firm belief and moments of profound doubt, and much in between.

'Death and dying offer an opportunity to see ourselves up close, with our defences exposed,' offers Smith (2015, p.86). In the midst of physical and emotional vulnerability we may see, all too clearly, the world we inhabit, and feel utterly unable to make the changes we might crave. This clarity, as my clients have often reflected, can be intensely frightening and profoundly liberating. Suddenly, they are speaking another language – a language that may disturb those around them if, indeed, it is heard at all. If we are sufficiently open, then it may be within counselling and/or accompaniment that clients may find the listening they need, and for which they yearn – essentially the space to feel, without censor, what they feel. *You think, crikey, can it be that bad? And it is that bad. It is that bad.'*

'The liminal spaces of mortality – those spaces at or above the psychological threshold of awareness – are often lit with dark, disturbing hues,' reflects Frommer (2005, p.482); it is to these liminal spaces that we are taken, I believe, when accompanying clients in the midst of illness and loss. I realise, of course, that however hard I try, it is impossible for me to truly understand at the level I would wish. Whether the fact is spoken or unspoken, we both know that our realities are different. In the light of significant illness – particularly illness with periods of respite or remission – this ongoing dissonance between worlds can be powerful, and deeply difficult to negotiate. *'It's my cancer…how can they possibly know…so don't tell me to feel better… don't tell me how I should feel!'* 'Dying patients do not seem to move in an orderly fashion through Elizabeth Kübler-Ross's (1969) five neat stages of denial, anger, bargaining, depression and acceptance. Many never get past denial,' argues O'Mahony (2016, p.121). Although I am not sure I concur with O'Mahony's bold claim here, I do find myself wondering about the impact of our cultural and societal obsession with happiness and success, and our seemingly perpetual avoidance of speaking of our innate vulnerability.

'The journey towards the truth is invariably painful,' offers Collingwood (2013, p.110), particularly, perhaps, within a culture that largely appears to function on denial, and within which 'people are medicating themselves by the millions in order to appear normal' (Granek 2014, p.63). We exist, therefore, in a somewhat surreal vacuum of our own collaborative making. Knowing our human fragility, and yet maintaining a communal silence that ostensibly denies such. It is almost as if none of us dare to speak first, for fear of being accused of bursting the bubble and plunging us all into an alternate dimension. So we hold our collective breath. Waiting. '"Are you better now?" they inquire kindly, in all innocence. "Of course I'm not," I want to say, "This is a life sentence. This is a vocation. It cannot be dismissed as comfortably as that!"' (Kerr 2013, p.159). This is a place of great aloneness, inevitably heightened by our silence. We let each other down. Life ebbs away, taking with it those people and places that are precious to us, caught in the slipstream.

'Why is it so often the case that we fully experience and value the now when we become aware that we are about to lose it?' asks Frommer (2005, p.480). *'Where am I? Who am I? What am I going through? What do I want out of the rest of my life now?' 'Should I be this upset?'* These, among many others, are the questions that perhaps tend 'to erupt at three in the morning' (Yalom 2008, p.11) – moments of the greatest aloneness, the strongest yearning and the deepest fear. No one can do this for us, and nothing can take it away. These are experiences that crash against the ordinary and the everyday, mocking our preoccupation with plans, and hopes, and dreams. This, for me, is the total pain, as defined by Saunders (2006), and is suffering at its most profound.

Bearing witness

'Those who have suffered,' argues O'Mahony (2016) 'are regarded as having a special moral authority' (p.205) – and what, I wonder, might this alleged authority prompt? Are we, as witnesses, drawn to protect and to soothe, rather than to encounter? Does our empathy begin to look rather more like sympathy? Might our congruence assume a different form in the face of physical pain and/or disability, and do we, therefore, cease to maintain parity within our counselling or accompaniment?

Bearing witness within such terrains can be intensely emotionally demanding, taking us, as Heath (2014) suggests, 'to the limit of our capacity to tolerate pain and anxiety'. However, she goes on to emphasise that 'we need to have the resources to do so because otherwise we are at risk of wanting our clients to achieve closure so that we feel more comfortable' (p.297). We might also find ourselves in the place of blaming or pathologising clients, claiming they are asking too much and/or becoming dependent, whereas, in reality, they are simply asking for what they need and it is we who are running away. Therapeutic accompaniment within this realm cannot be anything other than challenging, and the need for sensitive supervision remains paramount. As listeners, our capacity to tolerate chaos and confusion is critical.

Witnessing someone begin the immense process of adjusting to a body and a future that is no longer quite recognisable is profound and deeply moving. If I no longer know myself, then what? Can we dare to grieve for (or even acknowledge) those parts of us we never really knew existed until they made their presence known through their demise? Clients may hold a level of detachment with regard to the changes their bodies endure, or they may allow themselves to fully express the anger and frustration they feel, asking for the care, tenderness and compassion for which their bodies (and indeed spirits) may be crying out. They may do both, and far more besides. Adelbratt and Strang (2000, p.505) speak of periods within which a [client] 'vacillates between [denial and acceptance]. They are aware of their situation, but at the same time they deny it.' How much reality we actually have the capacity to tolerate is arguable, perhaps. but holding such truths closely to us, however they are shaped, is a uniquely demanding process.

'We cannot ultimately protect our [clients] from the pain of being alive' any more, of course, than we can protect ourselves, 'but we can help them to feel less alone in it, or, more accurately, to feel accompanied while they experience their aloneness' (Frommer 2005, p.496). I wonder, however, if some of our attempts to offer a salve to those in pain are really vain attempts at soothing ourselves? Through offering our clients comfort, connection and contact, we perhaps reassure ourselves that we are not alone in the universe. Do we offer a powerfully persuasive level of relating where the goal is to be met ourselves, rather than offer a space within which the other may experience, more fully, their individuality (Bazzano 2013)?

'There are places where our pain merges with our patients' pain, mixes, and turns into a single entity,' reflects Bonwitt. 'Quite possibly, there is no other way to remain within them' (2008, pp.231–232). But as much as proponents of relational depth may argue for the gift and healing of such intimate encounter, it can be deeply demanding for our clients – especially if 'to be seen' draws them into realms wherein they fear exposure, threat or rejection. Our defences have a critical role to play at times, perhaps. 'Being numb may be preferable to feeling pain, anxiety and sadness,' suggests Henry (2011, p.283). I have also, at times, worked with clients whose illness meant it was difficult, if not impossible, for them to cry, the energy involved demanding too much physical and emotional strength. I hold my empathy with the lightest of touches at times, acutely aware of the potential for overwhelm. We walk delicate edges here, and must not underestimate the emotional or spiritual impact of being in psychological contact with one another. As Heath reminds us, we hold an 'ethical responsibility to do no harm' (2014, p.297).

'Today, people want constant equilibrium,' argues Moore. 'They want every day to be a normal one' (2010, p.77). Often, and instinctively perhaps, our tendency is to flee from loss and grief; occasionally, we may fall completely into it. Far less often, perhaps, do we have the courage, or the capacity, to simply sit with it? If this reluctant by nature, how do we truly witness, with integrity, the pain of those who begin to learn the texture of their mortality? 'Be a merciful presence,' suggests Yoder (2011, p.89), but what does that really mean, and do we really have the capacity? We avoid taking the time and space, or perhaps, more disturbingly, we lack the inclination to truly reflect on our practice – to catch the shadows, to dare to look into our own abysses and to feel the edges of our own grief. 'For the most part,' challenges Yalom (2008, p.8), 'therapists avoid working directly with death anxiety. Perhaps it is because they are reluctant to face their own.' Am I? Are you? Are we deeply failing our clients because we dare not risk our own 'staring at the sun' (Yalom 2008)?

'One participant' in Axelsson et al.'s (2012) study described not knowing whether the care professionals were cowards, or considerate, when they avoided talking of his vulnerable illness situation (p.2154). This feels so critical. Are we cowards within this realm, or do we tread with delicacy? Is it possible to tell the difference, I wonder? Do we deceive ourselves into believing that we are being respectful, when the reality is that we are scared – scared of drawing too close to a realm that stirs profound pain for us? Do we then abandon one another at a time when we might most desperately need to be accompanied? The depth and quality of our presence is crucial here. 'Some...had tried to talk about end of life and death, but felt that their concerns were pushed away. Therefore, they kept existential thoughts to themselves, and everyday life was carried on trying to be as usual' (Axelsson *et al.* 2012, p.2153); *'They wanted to pretend they were still fighting it – so underneath pretty much just sort of hollow really.'* When everything is far from 'usual', the impact of this emotional/psychological incongruence may be profound and far-reaching. Holding the immensity of such existential crisis beneath the illusion of outward normality can cause immense pain and provoke deep depression – sometimes desperation. It is also utterly exhausting: *'I played the cancer card because there was nothing else to play.'* 'The world has destabilised,' asserts Heath (2014), 'and therefore the person has' (p.296). And, in the midst of this confusion, messages from those around us can profoundly heighten the pain experienced and the pressure felt: *'Everyone's telling you to make the most of that final year.'* What might that even mean?

'I have turned that knob and cracked that door. It is dark country – dark and penetrating' (Murphy 2013, p.72); perhaps, within such 'dark and penetrating country', 'connection is paramount... Get close in any way that feels appropriate. Speak from your heart. Reveal your own fears. Improvise. Hold the suffering one in any way that gives comfort,' urges Yalom (2008, p.130). Easy to urge, but far harder to offer, perhaps? The more I counsel within this realm, the more I question my capacity. 'Out of the sharing of our vulnerability, empathy grows,' offers Mayne (2006, p.245). Central to my commitment to my clients is my determination to face my own chaos: to sit in the darkness of my own experience, grapple with my confusion, fight my battles. Counterintuitive it may be, but if we really want to learn how to accompany others in loss and grief, the only real answer, surely, is to deeply feel it ourselves.

Summary

I am acutely aware that this chapter has been written from a place of considerable unknowing. As close as we may stand to our clients, we are still 'just watching' (Sontag 2003, p.105). The challenge for us, I believe, is how might such watching transform itself into a true witnessing? The closer we draw to an open and clear acknowledgement of our own grief, the more we might move toward a fuller being with another. Do we watch with the depth and understanding of having truly faced aspects of our own loss? Or do we watch while hoping that, through such, we will somehow be granted immunity? 'I urge you not to distract yourself,' offers Yalom (2008); 'keep in mind the advantage of remaining aware of death, of hugging its shadow close to you' (pp.146–147), for *as good as we are as professionals...there's something about sometimes getting pulled up sharp personally that actually makes us better at what we're doing.'*

As powerful and poignant as these encounters can become, do we, in our accompaniment, stand in danger of falling into the trap of listening for *profundity* rather than *reality* in those who talk with us? 'Death, as I have seen it,' reflects O'Mahony (2016, p.236), 'is more often marked by pain, fear, boredom and absurdity than it is by dignity, spirituality and meaning. What are we to do?' *'It might be the diagnosis that brings the client into the room but that's not what we end up talking about.'* Our own relationship with death and dying is so critical here. How close to those edges are we willing to go ourselves? Do we allow ourselves to be bored, afraid or hurt, or do we create cosiness within our practice? I both need and fear the challenge of walking the edges with my clients, my students and my colleagues, strongly believing that I am indeed far 'more human when [my] defences are shattered' (Pizer 2009, p.80). The more robust I am, the less sensitively I feel I am attuned to the lives and the pains of those I am with. This is the point of balance, perhaps, the delicate edge. Do we only find this out when we encounter it? Is this the essence of working at the threshold? Is everything else too safe and too restrictive?

'The story of a death is intimate, scary, huge,' states Roiphe (2016, p.15). One of the most memorably huge stories I have been privileged to witness was with a client who drew me, frequently, to edges and thresholds. Such was her determination not to lose contact with herself that she walked, often, 'up to the edge of incomprehensible chaos' (Roy 2010, p.76) – a chaos that was, at times, almost unbearable for her. I was frequently in awe of her daring. It was not, however, that she necessarily always chose to be so, for she frequently found herself flung into those places. As invulnerable as we may sometimes feel ourselves to be, we are all at the mercy of our physicality. The distortion and disappearance of my vision tells me that, once again, I am on the edge of a migraine. A pain I have very little control over, and absolutely no choice within. I wait the aura out until my vision returns as, up to this point, it always has. I am acutely aware that I am powerless to control this process. We have little choice when it comes to our physicality.

Moving through the 'inevitable vicissitudes of living' (Murphy 2013, p.74). I grow into my older age. I change, and life changes around me. 'People generally die in the same manner in which they have lived,' offers Yoder (2011), 'Personality, values and lifestyle typically remain consistent through the dying process' (p.142). This both reassures and frightens me in equal measure. Again, I find myself in tears. Is this solely my midlife battle with hormones, or something more profound? Do I underestimate the impact of immersing myself in so many stories of dying? Everything feels more fragile through these months. I read of despair and hope, of people dying in the most unimaginably awful places with very little around them to comfort or to hold. I frequently wonder how I might react to my own terminal diagnosis. How desperately anguished would I feel to have to say goodbye to those I love?

And, all the while, the debates and discussions continue to rage. What is assisted dying anyway? What does 'choice' mean within end-of-life care? How might I begin to die with dignity? 'Death is occurring in each moment of life,' offers Smith (2015, p.195), 'We are not the same person we were a moment ago, nor does anything in the universe maintain itself for even an instant.' The British Association for Counselling and Psychotherapy's Ethical Framework (BACP 2016) suggests 'courage' as one of the moral qualities to which we are 'strongly encouraged to aspire'. Courage indeed to face, with our clients and for ourselves, the most profound and intimate of all griefs. Beyond the remit and capacity of the '50-minute hour' perhaps. Beautifully described by Sullivan and Mason (2006) thus: 'As you move further, to the back row of the theatre, there's a softer light that illuminates your world' (p.121). This softer light, however, might not necessarily always feel very soft and will almost certainly demand another level of courage entirely – a courage that compels us to go deep and challenges us to keep our eyes open as we do.

Chapter 7

Spirituality and Sexual Abuse

Valda Swinton

Introduction

Sexual abuse has been prevalent and prominent in the news over recent years. Counsellors and spiritual accompaniers will almost certainly encounter the issue of sexual abuse in their journeying alongside others. The high-profile nature of the abuse, sometimes perpetrated by celebrities, and the period of time over which the abuse took place can affect the individual's ability to move forward from the abuse. What has been in the news has had a knock-on effect for individuals who have been abused, encouraging them to come forward and disclose their abuse. In this chapter, I will be addressing the effects of sexual abuse on an individual's spirituality. I will explore the impact that abuse has on the person, and on those who would seek to accompany them to find 'peace'.

In my experience, it is difficult to actually listen to the voices of trauma and pain without being indelibly changed by that experience. When I was a trainee counsellor, in order to gain experience, I volunteered in an organisation that worked with survivors of sexual abuse. In hindsight, I still view that experience as the most profound and life-changing during that period of my life. I felt that going through that process had an impact on my view of the world. I felt that I lost my innocence and developed a heightened sense that anyone could be a sexual abuser. I became more aware of the need to listen, and be open, to what children relate, and to see or hear cues that may otherwise have been missed.

Another personal experience that is important here was gained from supervising a trainee counsellor who was working with someone who was sexually abused by a family member in childhood. The trainee was so personally affected by listening to the voice of the victim of this trauma in the counselling room that when he came to supervision I vicariously experienced the trauma in the supervision room – so traumatic was the experience for both of us. Sexual abuse has an impact on spirituality, with individuals either turning to spiritual beliefs and practices or experiencing intense struggles with the idea of spirituality. The question that some survivors could be asking of God is 'Where are you?' or 'Where were you?' Or, conversely, God could have been seen as the only one that was there (Murray-Swank and Pargament 2005). The experience of being sexually abused can have a life-transforming effect upon the person. So powerfully can the impact of this experience be that it may take years for the individual to disclose the abuse – and, in some cases, the abuse is never disclosed. The impact of being sexually abused on spirituality for the individual can vary depending on the identity of the abuser or when the abuse occurred.

Background and definitions of abuse

Draucker and Martsolf (2006) refer to the fact that the sexual abuse of children was denied for a long time by public health and mental health professionals. Indeed, Freud even dismissed the significance of incest, and suggested that these traumatic experiences were the cause of hysteria. To protect the family structure, he did not identify that abuse could be perpetrated by fathers or mothers. In response to peer pressure, he eventually claimed that the reports of sexual abuse were incestuous fantasies rather than actual sexual abuse experiences. He had first discussed how women were suffering from trauma resulting from sexual contact in childhood. There were two aspects to the experiences: the events were so terrible that they (1) left an emotion-charged residue in the psyche and (2) produced altered states of consciousness which encased the trauma. This process involved the generation of powerful emotions that threatened to overwhelm the person's ability to function. This was the first study of trauma pointing to disturbing aspects of Western family life. Freud's 'seduction theory' was received with a mixture of outrage and fascination that had considerable impact on him, and which led to him abandoning his theory. This setback had a profound effect on the acceptance of sexual abuse in childhood. In his work with women, Freud discovered the horrors that were being committed in the family. However, the full extent was not realised until the 1960s, with feminism and women questioning their role. Unfortunately, Freud's repudiation of his seduction theory made possible the continued denial of the prevalence of sexual abuse by professionals and the public at large. Yet now researchers highlight that sexual abuse occurs more frequently than was originally believed, with the NSPCC reporting that almost three-quarters (72 per cent) of sexually abused children did not tell anyone about the abuse at the time, 27 per cent told someone later, while around a third (31 per cent) still had not told anyone about their experience(s) by early adulthood. Police recorded over 23,000 sex offences against children aged under 18 years in England and Wales between April 2010 and March 2011 (NSPCC 2013).

Definitions

Browne and Finkelhor (1986) highlight that childhood sexual abuse has two features that are overlapping interactions: (1) sexual behaviour that is coerced and imposed on a child; (2) sexual behaviour between a child and a mature person, with, or without, coercion. Sexual abuse is described as anything that may have seemed sexual – for example, a request or invitation to do something sexual, or being shown someone's genitals. It appears that definition and categorisation is still difficult, but one such attempt at a definition is:

> The involvement of developmentally immature children and adolescents in sexual actions which they cannot fully comprehend; the inability to give informed consent, and which violate the social taboos of social roles. (Kempe and Kempe 1984)

There are problems with any definition that does not take account of threat or force. Also, some acts are only abusive because they are not socially acceptable, and we have to consider that in different cultures some acts may be acceptable. Hall and Lloyd (1993, p.3) highlight that the overall definition should include:

- betrayal of trust and responsibility
- abuse of power

- indication of the wide range of sexual activity

- use of threat and/or force, and the child's perception of this

- undermining personal resilience and psychological functioning that consequently affect interpersonal relationships and sexual health.

Characteristics of sexual abuse

As we have seen above, the nature of sexual abuse can create difficulties for the child, which can continue into adulthood. In addition, Sanderson (2011) states that there are various factors such as the following.

Age the abuse began

This is highly significant because the younger the victim, the less likely they are to have the capacity to reason in a way that would prevent them internalising the distorted messages fed to them by the abuser.

The gender of the individual/relationship to and identity of the abuser

Sexual abuse by females is still taboo and more hidden than abuse by men. Most abuse is perpetrated by fathers, or father figures, or by those in some position of authority. A small percentage of abusers are female. The more the abuser is involved in the life of the victim, and the more that is invested in this relationship, the greater the impact. One of the falsities in relation to child sexual abuse has been that it is just men who sexually abuse children. Denov (2003) helps us to understand the underlying issues that give rise to this outrage when we are faced with the fact that women do sexually abuse children. First, there is a common belief that women are 'incapable of committing sexual offences' (p.3). Furthermore, the idea of a sexually abusive woman does not fit with our sense of 'femininity', because this idea conjures up a picture of someone who is nurturing, and all the other adjectives that we could add to what a being mother means to us. Denov (2003) states that it is culturally difficult to grapple with the idea that women sexually abuse children. To compound this issue, those who report that they have been sexually abused by a female may find that their abuser will not be prosecuted. Hetherton and Beardsall (1988) state that this area is under-reported, and they focus our attention on the cultural bias that affects society's recognition of the fact that women sexually abuse children. This bias may have an influence on the professionals who make the recommendations that could bring an end to the abuse, and to the perpetrator being prosecuted. Sadly, one of Hetherton and Beardsall's hypotheses was that child protection professionals (social workers and police) were less likely to take seriously the abuse perpetrated by females, in contrast to abuse perpetrated by males.

Allegations of child sexual abuse and the Church

When sexual abuse is perpetrated by the clergy, or in a religious or spiritual context, then the impact on the person's sense of God, their religion or their spirituality is much more deeply wounding. Pargament, Murray-Swank and Mahoney (2008, p.398) highlight that 'where we find trauma, we often find spirituality', because individuals find help and comfort from their faith during times of crisis. Therefore, if spirituality becomes part of the problem rather than an avenue to find help, support and comfort, it is not hard to imagine the negative impact that this may have on the individual who has been sexually abused, either by the clergy or by someone within their faith community.

Pargament et al. (2008) define spirituality as not just about a set of beliefs, but about our search for meaning and purpose in life, which involves a search for the sacred. It is the sacred that lies behind religion, pointing to the importance that many people place on this domain of their experience. Sexual abuse perpetrated within a spiritual environment may shatter everything the person held dear or hinder the development of a strong spiritual foundation to the individual's life. It is a violation on a number of levels, like the abuse that is perpetrated by fathers and father figures. As the clergy could be viewed as God's representative on earth, Pargament et al. (2008) refer to the idea that it is as if it was God who committed the abuse. For some individuals who have been abused in a spiritual context, rather than giving up on spirituality completely, a consequence of being abused is that the individual may subsequently embark on a spiritual journey to discover a new spiritual home (Crisp 2007).

When abuse is reported, Church leaders need to realise that insurance companies may have a vested interest in not prosecuting sex offenders. Therefore, it might be prudent to keep quiet. Law firms and insurance companies might believe that this is in the best interest of their clients. Abusive power structures can lead to situations where abuse is tolerated and sanctioned. Decisions can be based on what is best for the institution rather than the child (Vieth *et al.* 2012). Minton *et al.* (2016, p.1) discussed what they referred to as 'the role of group allegiances in contributing to the failure of institutions to appropriately respond to allegations of child sexual abuse'. This allegiance could play a part in the failure not just of the Church but of other institutions, whether hospitals, children's homes, the police and local authorities, to respond to the numerous reports that have come to light over the last few years. Minton *et al.* (2016) highlight the failures in their duty of care to those in their charge of religious, educational, charitable, sporting, health and correctional institutions. Sadly, the failure to respond appropriately to reported allegations is only the tip of the iceberg of the actual number of individuals who have been abused, as many cases of abuse are unreported. Members of some institutions have gone to 'significant lengths' in their effort to protect the reputation of the organisation, and thereby the perpetrators. This has been the situation in relation to the Church (Vieth *et al.* 2012).

Duration and frequency of the abuse

The abuse could have been a one-off, committed by a trusted adult, or may have occurred several times a week over a period of months or years. The regularity and period of the abuse, as well as the nature of the abuse, will add to the trauma of the experience.

The age of the child

For many sexually abused children, the abuse will have started before puberty. On the other hand, if the abuse occurred at an older age, then it is possible that a secure sense of the spiritual or a strong relationship with God may have already been established, which could have been a source of help and comfort to the individual (Gall 2006).

Age of the abuser/multiple abusers

The abuser is usually a lot older, or there could have been a number of abusers – as, for example, in ritual abuse.

What support was available

Having continuing support from family and friends when the abuse took place, and in later life, can help with processing the abuse. Sadly, the secret nature of sexual abuse means that the support is often not available (Sanderson 2011). Therefore, it is important at this stage to sound a note of caution, and to acknowledge that sexual abuse will affect individuals in different ways. For some individuals, it may be a devastating experience, whereas for others the impact might be less severe, with the above factors affecting the severity of the experience.

Obstacles to spiritual growth and development

In discussing the idea of spirituality and sexual abuse, Ganje-Fling and McCarthy (1996) state that spirituality provides a sense of meaning, a sense of hope, esteem and belonging for the individual (p.256). According to Crisp (2007), those who have been sexually abused have a negative image of self, and of God; they may have problems of low self-esteem and have little sense of their own value or worth, consequently believing that nothing good will ever come their way. This highlights how abuse negates the functions of spirituality. Crisp (2007), in referring to her own personal experience, writes, 'Of all the relationships in my life, one that has been among the most difficult is the relationship with myself' (p.303). Other obstacles to spirituality that abuse survivors have highlighted include a sense of unworthiness, distrust, anger, or guilt; and that they have lost their trust in the world and in God, especially if they were abused by a father figure (Ganje-Fling 2000). They experience continuing spiritual injury, distress and personal and spiritual alienation (Lawson *et al.* 1998). It appears that another impact of being sexually abused is that psychological and spiritual development may have halted at the age that the abuse occurred (Ganje-Fling and McCarthy 1996). The examples that Ganje-Fling and McCarthy (1996) give are that survivors' concepts of God, or Higher Power, may still be naïve; they may have an inability to conceptualise the idea of a spiritual force, and hold rigidity about the meaning of life as well as in their ideas about good and evil. Survivors may have a sense of mistrust, particularly around authority figures, and this mistrust may extend to God or to a Higher Power. Their feelings about the perpetrators can subsequently become their feelings about God. Consequently, there is difficulty in surrendering in faith to God, or a Higher Power, when abuse is what has been experienced before.

There could also be questions about the goodness of God, who did not intervene to prevent the abuse. Survivors may have lost their sense that there is any meaning or purpose to life. They may live with despair rather than hope about the future, as they may have a history of being defeated and have lost hope that life could be different. Responsibility may be misplaced from the perpetrator to the survivor, who then takes responsibility for the abuse. Forgiveness may also be another conflicting issue, coupled with early experiences of religious upbringing. The conflicts may arise because of strict fundamentalist religious backgrounds that may encourage individuals to either ignore or even support acts of abuse. With hindsight, some individuals may experience their backgrounds as abusive, especially when the alleged abuse was perpetrated by a member of the clergy (Ganje-Fling and McCarthy 1996).

Spiritual struggles following sexual abuse have been reported in the literature (e.g. Gall 2006), which include difficulty with religious identity, anger with God, feeling abandoned by the deity, negative images of God and consequently spiritual isolation. Sexual abuse appears to affect the psychological, physical and spiritual health of victims of such abuse (Gall 2006). Sanderson (2011) adds that as well as having an impact on spiritual experiencing, sexual abuse can disrupt biological, emotional and intellectual functioning. To cope with the experience, many survivors disconnect from the abuse itself and the resulting painful feelings. The disconnection from self can have an even more far-reaching effect in that the disconnection then extends to their relationships with other people. The greatest impact is on the individual's sense of personal power and control, both internally and externally. Being sexually abused can also distort the person's sense of reality, and with the abuse comes a number of losses. One of these can be a loss of faith.

Pargament *et al.* (2008) state that one of the ways to discover divine qualities, such as the sacredness of existence, is through religious institutions, and the discovery of the sacred means that this can be something to draw on as a resource as the individual grows and develops. Therefore, the fact that most people discover the sacred in childhood means that sexual abuse in childhood may affect the process of spiritual discovery, which could negatively affect normal spiritual development (p.401). This may have a lasting impact on a relationship with God and the Church. The timing of the abuse, in terms of development, may be a major factor in the person's ability to use spirituality as a support in later life. It has been suggested that children who were abused at a younger age may experience disruption in their ability to develop a firm and unshakeable sense in a God that is kind. So, in adulthood, they are unlikely to look to God, or others, for spiritual support. If this relationship in childhood did not develop to enable the individual to see God as a source of support, particularly in times of stress or difficulty, then there would be no sense of a secure relationship. For those who accompany individuals who have been sexually abused, the following are important issues to consider.

Theories that account for the long-term effects of sexual abuse

Along with the traumatisation effects of sexual abuse, some other theories have been proffered for the enduring effects on the individual of their experience of being abused. In this section, I will explore in more detail a couple of the theories for the long-term effects (see other effects in Table 7.1).

Table 7.1: Summary of long-term consequences of child sexual abuse

Emotional reactions and self-perceptions	Physical consequences/ somatic complaints	Effects on social and sexual functioning
Guilt	Physical complaints	Abuse of self:
Anger and rage	Sleep disturbance	• self-mutilation and injury
Sadness and grief	Eating disorders	• suicidal attempts
Complete absence of emotional reaction	Perceptual disturbances	Substance abuse:
Depression	Flashbacks	• alcohol
Anxiety problems:	Nightmares/bad dreams	• drugs
• generalised anxiety	Out-of-body experiences	• tranquillisers
• panic attacks	Adolescent pregnancy	Compulsive and obsessional problems
• specific fears and phobias		Under-achievement in education and occupation
• pronounced startle response		Difficulty in sustaining positive experiences
Self-destructive behaviour		Confusion
Low self-esteem		Problems with trust
Shame and dissociation		Victim behaviour
Isolation and alienation		Further assault/revictimisation by husband or partners
Stigmatisation		General fear of men
Bad reactions to medical procedures:		Sexual problems:
• hospital admissions		• impaired sexual arousal
• gynaecological procedures		• difficulties with orgasm
• dental procedures		• lack of sexual motivation
		• lack of sexual satisfaction
		• guilt during sexual contact
		• vaginismus
		• pain during intercourse
		Interpersonal difficulties:
		• in relationships with men
		• in relationships with women
		Problems with touch
		Parenting problems – closeness and affection has sexual connotation

(collated from Hall and Lloyd 1993 and Browne and Finkelhor 1986)

Post-traumatic stress disorder (PTSD) model

To account for the long-terms effects of sexual abuse, clinicians and researchers have attempted to formulate models to help to explain the symptoms and effects that have been observed. The PTSD model appears to mirror some of the effects of childhood sexual abuse that are similar to the experience of war veterans. Sanderson (2006) says that this is the experience of a traumatic event that elicits symptoms of distress which lead to the re-experiencing of the trauma event in the form of flashbacks, dreams and nightmares. There is also avoidance behaviour in regard to stimuli associated with the trauma, as well as symptoms of increased arousal – for example, difficulty in falling asleep. Other effects may be:

- psychogenic amnesia

- reduced affect and numbing

- hyper-vigilance

- isolation

- anger

- stigmatisation

- intrusive recollections of the trauma

- physiological and psychological arousal symptoms (panic attacks or anxiety).

Sanderson (2006), in discussing the PTSD model, clarifies that this diagnosis accounts for many of the observed symptoms, but not for the full range – for example, cognitive effects. Although this diagnosis helps to clarify some of the effects in adult survivors, the PTSD model can only apply to some victims of child sexual abuse.

Traumagenic dynamics model

Finkelhor and Browne's (1985, pp.531–533) traumagenic dynamics model is seen as an alternative to the PTSD model, and suggests four traumagenic dynamics to explain the impact of abuse that results in this trauma. The model explains how sexual abuse can be analysed in four trauma-causing factors. It is the coming together of these four dynamics in the sexual abuse experience that makes the trauma of sexual abuse unique and different from other childhood traumas:

1. *Traumatic sexualisation:* This is when the child's sexuality is shaped in an inappropriate way, interpersonally and developmentally. The development of traumatisation could be because the individual is rewarded by the abuser for sexual behaviour that is inappropriate for the age of the child. The learning from this is to use sexual behaviour as manipulation to get other needs met. Traumatic sexualisation can occur because of the effort that is exerted to get the child to develop a sexual response, or the force that is used becoming associated with a fear of sexual contact in later life. The impact is that individuals emerge from the experience with inappropriate or unusual associations about sexual activity and sexuality.

2. *Betrayal:* This is the discovery that someone whom they have trusted, and on whom they depend, has betrayed their trust and caused them harm. They may feel manipulated through lies and through a distorted representation of what is an appropriate moral standard. Their needs have been disregarded; they have not been protected and they feel abandoned once the abuse has been disclosed. The sense of betrayal might be compounded because it has been a close family member, and disclosure of the abuse has been received with disbelief, blame or being ostracised.

3. *Stigmatisation:* This is to do with the negative perceptions that result from the experience – a sense of badness, shame or guilt – that is incorporated into the child's sense of self. The negativity could have been communicated by the abuser, other family members or by society generally. The stigmatisation could be through the child's own sense of right and wrong, which can be reinforced depending on the reaction once the abuse is disclosed.

4. *Powerlessness:* The child is rendered powerless by the overpowering of their will, desires and sense of efficacy. This powerlessness is repeatedly reinforced as the child's personal space and body is re-invaded, or compounded with the degree

of threat, force, coercion or manipulation that is exerted by the abuser. The sense of powerlessness could also be reinforced because of the child's sense of failure to prevent the abuse, or to be believed, and because they are trapped in a dependent relationship with the abuser. In addition, the power and authority of the abuser in commanding the child to participate through threats of serious harm to the child's family or pets, for example, is also disempowering. Feeling less disempowered occurs only if the child is able to bring the abuse to an end, or exert some control over the abusive situation.

Impact on journeying alongside another

False memory syndrome (FMS)

In accompanying someone alleging childhood sexual abuse, an important issue that needs to be taken into account is the debate surrounding the recovery of false memories. There is a risk that someone who is not very skilled in therapeutic or accompaniment work could unintentionally introduce material that might lead to them being accused of inducing the false memories in the client/accompanee. The idea of false memory syndrome was formed in response to the number of adults who accused their parents of childhood sexual abuse in the 1980s and 1990s. A coalition of those who considered they were falsely accused sprang up, and the False Memory Syndrome Foundation was established in the USA in 1992. The coalition was founded by two parents who felt aggrieved that their daughter broke off contact with them. The situation came about because their daughter had recently acquired beliefs that she had been abused as a child. These 'memories' came to light through participation in 'memory recovery' therapy, and this was cited as the cause of the problem. There is controversy about the empirical basis on which this idea was founded, and heated debate ensued on both sides. Adding fuel to the fire of the debate at the time were the people who retracted their accusations about being sexually abused by a parent. Also, there was agreement that individuals could be influenced by abuse literature. In addition, particular forms of therapy may develop beliefs about a personal history of abuse. Therefore, it is necessary to take into consideration the process whereby new memories promote beliefs, as opposed to new beliefs promoting memories. This is an area in which an individual must exercise great care when journeying alongside another.

Vicarious traumatisation

My own experience of having trained and worked in this area, as well as the effect on the trainee counsellor referred to earlier in this chapter, has relevance for those working with, or accompanying, anyone who has experienced traumatic events. The idea of vicarious traumatisation was introduced by McCann and Pearlman (1990) to describe the effects of trauma on those living or working with clients who have experienced trauma. The idea was formed to describe the development of a syndrome in therapists who were working with incest survivors. The early work in this area focused on traumatisation of therapists listening to stories of abuse. It was not only from listening to but from witnessing the horror of their clients. Vicarious traumatisation is a label that is attached to any helper who hears stories about traumatic events. This is also referred to as secondary traumatic stress theory. The idea is that there are chronic stressors caused from being in close contact with, and from being emotionally connected to, a traumatised person. These are trauma-like symptoms that develop in those working with what could be referred to as 'complex trauma', which results from hearing the terrible stories of clients' traumatisation. Journeying with someone who is telling and retelling horrific events can be a very powerful and distressing experience. Vicarious traumatisation brings about a transformation of the helper's inner experiencing, resulting from empathic engagement with the other's trauma material. This might affect one's ability to sustain empathic engagement. Staying with such a process can be very difficult, and we may find ourselves putting up defences in order to contain our own distress in order to protect ourselves from what is being heard. There is recognition that a person could be traumatised by hearing about harm to a loved one, as has been included in the *Diagnostic and Statistical Manual of Mental Disorders* from 1980 onwards. There is a specific context:

- Intense environments where stories of traumatisation constitute the majority of the person's work.

- The work of therapists or accompaniers mainly consists of listening to stories of sexual and physical abuse.

- These stories can be horrific and painful to hear, think about or imagine, especially when listening to the experience of the child who becomes prey to the lies and deceit of the perpetrator.

This was the realisation in the therapeutic community that therapists can develop trauma-like symptoms. Some signs/symptoms include:

- nightmares
- hyper-vigilance
- having flashbacks
- avoidance of emotions
- displaying more anger/aggression
- becoming cynical.

Specific change in the therapist or accompanier include:

- disrupted frame of reference, psychological needs, and cognitive schemas
- diminished self-capacities
- impaired ego resources
- alterations in sensory experiences (e.g. intrusive imagery, dissociation and depersonalisation)
- changes in identity, worldview – becoming negative
- disrupted beliefs/relationships
- unmanageable emotions
- indecision.

General changes in the therapist or accompanier include:

- no time or energy for oneself
- disconnection from loved ones
- social withdrawal
- increased sensitivity to violence
- general despair, hopelessness and nightmares.

It appears that a parallel process takes place through exposure to the level of horror in client's stories. In their survey of women psychotherapists, Brady *et al.* (1999) report that vicarious traumatisation and spirituality are linked directly. This is because damage to one's spiritual life is one of the possible outcomes of the traumatisation. On the other hand, faith could emerge as stronger and more resilient, and as a way of coping with the effects of vicarious traumatisation. Therefore, understanding the relationship between vicarious traumatisation and spirituality is important for those who accompany individuals who have been sexually abused. It is important that those who walk alongside individuals who have been abused should have a clear understanding of their own spirituality. They should also have personally addressed 'existential' issues around the questions about the meaning of life and suffering.

Transference/countertransference

Another issue that needs to be taken into consideration when working in this area is transference and countertransference. Transference takes place when the survivor starts to react to the listener as though they were the perpetrator of the abuse. To be listened to can be powerful and seductive, and this might be the first time that the individual has told the story of their experience. This investment of oneself, one's time and one's energy to listen and hear the story might provoke a sense of dependency on the part of the survivor of abuse. The nature of the experience of being vulnerable may remind the abused individual of similar important individuals in their childhood. The listener can be seen by the abused individual in a similar way to the way in which they saw the original perpetrator – as the one having power to control, to harm or to abuse them. We have to be careful in such situations that we do not then develop powerful countertransference in response to what is being transferred, which can touch on deep-seated issues in our own lives. Wisdom is required so that the transference reaction of the client does not draw us into performing a role that is out of our own awareness. There is a need for objectivity and to not feel personally threatened or attacked. Sanderson (2006) says that releasing feelings in an environment that is safe and supportive can be a means for the individual to find healing. Being aware of the transference process might help the therapist or accompanier to not feel threatened by 'acted out' behaviour. Brady *et al.* (1999, p.4) assert that issues of 'countertransference are not less real in the therapeutic area of spirituality than they are in other clinical areas'. To hear and to witness the horrifying experiences recounted by survivors can leave an indelible mark on the listener.

As mentioned earlier, Ganje-Fling and McCarthy (1996, p.253) state that the functions of spirituality are about meaning, hope, esteem and belonging. When journeying alongside another who has suffered sexual abuse, the work is therefore about how these functions of spirituality can be restored. How do we enable individuals who have been sexually abused to have the courage to look within when they may be experiencing conflict with any sense of spirituality, especially if their development was arrested at the time the abuse occurred? They may not feel safe with anyone who could be regarded as an authority figure. Ganje-Fling and McCarthy (1996) report that, psychologically and spiritually, individuals may blame themselves for the abuse and therefore struggle with any sense of spiritual worthiness or the ability to forgive. Their sense of unworthiness may be deeply imbedded, and there may be issues of power, whether it is with the authority figure that is the helper, or with a Higher Power who could be another potential abuser. In addition, trust issues could surface, or any form of change could engender fear with the need for reassurance. Ganje-Fling and McCarthy (1996) found that clients who had been traumatised by abuse also present with a great fear of death, with no understanding of the reason for this fear. They suggest two reasons for this fear: (1) their birth family did not place enough emphasis on the value of life; and (2) those who were hurt by those who gave them life may then believe that life has no real value.

It is important that individuals are enabled to identify any spiritual experiences from childhood, or since, and also their own spiritual power. Researchers have found that spirituality can play an important role in the present adjustment of individuals, and that the greater the importance survivors place on their spirituality, the greater the impact on personal growth. It appears that survivors could experience fewer depressive moods and could experience a sense of resolution of their abuse history. The survivor who has a greater sense of personal spirituality is the one with the key ingredient in enabling their own well-being (Gall *et al.* 2007). The individual may feel a mixture of ambiguity in desiring to regain a sense of spirituality or relationship with God, or Higher Power. They may have difficulty in responding positively to images of God, or in trusting in the idea of God as loving. In addition, they may place the blame for the abuse on God or a

Higher Power, or feel angry with God for what has happened to them (Crisp 2007; Murray-Swank and Pargament 2005). There may also be difficulties with issues of forgiveness of self and the perpetrator (Turell and Thomas 2001). Finally, survivors need to be provided with an avenue for addressing problems of spirituality, so that they do not become spiritually disenchanted, if this has not already occurred.

Summary

This chapter has explored issues that are relevant when working with individuals who have experienced sexual abuse. I began by giving a glimpse of my own experience of working therapeutically in this area. Sexual abuse can result in deep and lasting trauma at a psychological and spiritual level, not just to the survivors but also to those who would listen to their voices of trauma. It is important to be aware of the impact that listening may have on the listener's life and worldview. Those who have been abused may tell stories about journeys that have been fraught with spiritual distress, and stories of lives and personal relationships that have been marred by their experience. Also, those who have been abused by father figures, whether in the Church or in their family, may experience greater trauma. The trauma of sexual abuse may be compounded when the abuse is disclosed if the victim is not believed. In addition, the gender of the perpetrator may be a factor in whether the abuse is believed and the perpetrator prosecuted. Although there may be a personal impact on those who work therapeutically in this area, the positive aspects of working with survivors to recover a sense of well-being may outweigh any negative aspects. Being in supervision and having good self-care are crucial to surviving this work, either as a counsellor or spiritual accompanier.

Chapter 8

Trauma and Spiritual Growth

Nikki Kiyimba

In his widely acclaimed book *When Bad Things Happen to Good People*, Rabbi Harold Kushner (2007) candidly discussed the challenge to his faith when his son died prematurely from an unusual disease that caused rapid aging. His belief that God was all-powerful, just, fair and good was badly shaken, and he was forced to re-examine everything he thought he knew to be true. When a trauma happens, long-held beliefs are suddenly brought into question, and a process of psychological and existential crisis can ensue. The crisis can force processes of personal re-evaluation and learning (Bray 2013). In the research conducted on trauma to date, however, the social, psychological and physical aspects have received far more interest and attention than the spiritual dimension of trauma (Pargament, Desai and McConnell 2006). Nevertheless, in order to fully understand the processes of post-traumatic growth, it is important to consider the role that spirituality plays in any individual growth that occurs following trauma (O'Rourke, Tallman and Altmaier 2008). The spiritual domains of experience are thought to be influential on an individual's growth in the aftermath of stressful life events (Bray 2010). This chapter begins by examining what trauma is and what spirituality is, and then moves on to engage with the interesting topic of post-traumatic growth (PTG), particularly the dimension of spiritual change that has been highlighted as one of the facets of PTG.

Trauma and its impact

Erikson defined trauma as a 'blow to the psyche that breaks through one's defenses so suddenly and with such brutal force that one cannot react to it effectively' (1976, p.156). When post-traumatic stress disorder (PTSD) was first conceptualised as a psychiatric disorder, 'traumatic experiences' were described as events 'outside the range of usual human experience' (American Psychiatric Association 1980, p.250). Unfortunately, however, as our modern world hurtles forward with an ever-increasing magnitude of difficult and 'traumatic' events, this phrase is becoming less and less salient. We live in times when earthquakes, floods, wars, political unrest causing thousands to flee their homes as refugees, and terrorist attacks are much more commonplace, not to mention the violence and abuse that is a part of many people's everyday lives. This means that the world is rapidly becoming one in which events that may be defined as 'traumatic' are now more often within the range of usual human experience.

However much more frequently they occur, the events themselves are still experienced as traumatic by those who are caught up in them. The evidence of this lies in part within epidemiological studies that are indicating an increase in PTSD to the extent that it is now a major worldwide health concern (Brunello *et al.* 2001). One theory of what happens psychologically when a person encounters a traumatic experience is the 'shattered assumptions' model that was proposed by Janoff-Bulman (2010). This theory is based on the premise that when a trauma occurs many previously held beliefs about the world, self and others can be radically challenged. These changes occur through three distinct, but not necessarily mutually exclusive, processes which are 'strength through suffering, psychological preparedness and existential reevaluation' (Janoff-Bulman 2004, p.30). It is this latter element of existential re-evaluation that is of particular interest and focus. In other words, post-trauma, the person is in a process of what Attig (1996) refers to as 'relearning the world'. Whether the cause is losing a home in a tornado or losing a limb in a terrorist attack, the shock and horror of the experience can leave its victims reeling, not only from the physical impact but also existentially, as they try to make sense of the world in the aftermath of these events. Where people may have felt safe, or have felt that life was reasonably predictable before the event, new questions arise about self, the world and others, and how to relate to each of these aspects of life. Many experience acute pain, loss, disorientation, anger, fear, confusion and a host of conflicting thoughts, as previously held beliefs and assumptions about the world are shaken to the core. In the midst of this turmoil, people who have experienced trauma go through a process of needing to re-learn how the world is, by reintegrating this new information into previously existing schemas. Inevitably, this process is painful and difficult, as huge inner adjustments have to be made. However, through this struggle, and certainly not instead of it, many people experience what has come to be known as 'post-traumatic growth'.

Post-traumatic growth

The possibility of positive growth arising from the struggle with highly stressful events is one that fits well with emerging models of therapy that emphasise strength and resilience (Park and Helgeson 2006). Post-traumatic growth (PTG) is a term used to describe the positive change that some survivors report in the aftermath of trauma, and relates to changes in five areas: relating to others, new possibilities, personal strength, appreciation of life and spiritual change (Tedeschi and Calhoun 1996). The focus of this chapter is on the particular aspect of PTG that is referred to as 'spiritual change'. In developing a measure of PTG called the post-traumatic growth inventory (PTGI), Tedeschi and Calhoun (1996) included two items within the 21-question inventory to measure religious and spiritual change. The first item measures the spiritual aspect of PTG in terms of a connection to the transcendent that had not existed before (Tedeschi, Park and Calhoun 1998). The second item measures religious affiliation as a way to interpret the form that this new connection with the transcendent takes (Tedeschi and Calhoun 2006). It is acknowledged that the categories are not mutually exclusive, and since the development of the PTGI, Calhoun and Tedeschi's more recent work (2006) places less emphasis on religion and focuses more on existential questions. There is now an understanding that individuals can experience the spiritual aspects of PTG irrespective of religious beliefs (Calhoun et al. 2010). This follows recognition that the existential awakening that can occur during the time of adjustment following a traumatic experience may not be categorised by the person experiencing it as 'spiritual' per se. Instead, he or she may experience this shift as a difference in thinking about their priories in life, or recognition of the value of their close relationships, for example.

The trauma survivor often has to come to terms with the fact that the world can be unsafe, unjust and unpredictable. However, these inevitable adjustments in making sense of the world and changes in self-perception that appear to come along as part of the process of post-trauma experiences are best not thought of in dichotomous terms such as bad or good, debilitating or empowering, harmful or life-affirming. Rather, these two seemingly opposite, or contradictory, positions can be experienced simultaneously; pain and growth can co-exist. The threat of the trauma exposes the sense of human vulnerability and mortality, and, at the same time, the process of finding inner resilience to survive the trauma sends a strong message to the self that is both positive and empowering. Cognitions about oneself in the processing time after a trauma may be both: 'I am more vulnerable than I thought, but much stronger than I ever imagined' (Calhoun and Tedeschi 2014, p.5). Vulnerability and a sense of human frailty and mortality can co-exist with a new understanding of one's strength, resilience and ability to cope with what previously may have been imagined as impossible circumstances.

In her study of the impact of a terrorist bombing of the Murrah Building in Oklahoma in 1995, Fisher (2006) reported that there were greater levels of PTG in those who met the criteria for PTSD than those who did not. What this indicates is that where the response to the trauma was more debilitating (i.e. those who were clinically diagnosed with PTSD), the same people also demonstrated higher levels of PTG. Those individuals, despite still experiencing painful symptoms, also reported 'considerable positive change particularly in appreciating life, feelings of self-reliance, and significantly stronger religious faith' (p.318). Thus, the notion that PTG and post-traumatic stress may be mutually exclusive is actually unfounded; in reality, those who experience the most severe post-traumatic stress are the very same people for whom there is a considerable chance of also experiencing greater PTG.

Spirituality and spiritual struggle

One definition of spirituality is a 'belief in a power apart from one's own existence and implies a connection with a universal force transcending everyday sense-bound reality' (Connor, Davidson and Lee 2003, p.487). Where spirituality relates to belief, religion tends to refer to the rituals and social practices within a culture or community that provide the methods for attaining spirituality (Griffith and Griffith 2002). Although the expression of spirituality, through religious practices, is important, it is spirituality in its broadest sense that is the focus of this discussion, rather than the specific practices of religion. The definition of spirituality offered, which focuses on the central importance of belief, can appear rather static, as though belief is something that is fixed. However, it is suggested that a more holistic way of thinking about spirituality is to understand it more in terms of a process or journey wherein there is a search for meaning and purpose (e.g. Decker 1993; King, Speck and Thomas 2001). It is this aspect of searching for meaning that arguably most closely links definitions of spirituality with the thoughts, emotions and experiences that are pervasive in the aftermath of a trauma.

A sense of meaning in life and an unfolding of one's belief system might normally be considered to be an evolving process throughout life, as one assimilates new experiences and philosophies. However, in the face of trauma, this gradual process is apprehended and short-circuited, forcing the individual to re-evaluate their way of making sense of the world in the light of new and overwhelming information. The time of trauma is often when 'meaning may be created and found' (Tedeschi *et al.* 1998, p.4). An example of this is the story of an elderly man, deeply distressed after the death of his wife, who, when asked to reflect on how it would have been for his wife if he had been the one who died first, created a new meaning within his state of loss, which was that, by passing first, she had been saved from the grief and suffering that he was experiencing (North Hollywood 2000).

Spiritual beliefs can influence the way people react to illness and bereavement. Feelings of loss, abandonment, alienation, suffering, anger and dependency all come into play, in addition to concerns with forgiveness, peace, hope, grief and the meaning of life. Some individuals, in their search for meaning, might return to childhood religious beliefs, whereas others search for new expressions of spirituality (Waldfogel and Wolpe 1993). In whatever way a person reacts, there is often a degree of cognitive dissonance that occurs at least initially in the event of a trauma. One part of the mind is still holding on to prior assumptions about the world, about self and about other people, while simultaneously there are actual physical circumstances that may radically challenge those previously unquestioned beliefs.

This dilemma prompts a search for understanding and a reconstruction of the ways in which the person makes sense of things and finds meaning (Neimeyer 1998; Steffen and Coyle 2010).

Spirituality as a resilience factor in managing trauma

Spirituality is very important in the ways in which people cope with trauma and acute stress (Calhoun *et al.* 2000; Lau and Grossman 1997; Park, Cohen and Murch 1996; Waysmann, Schwarzwald and Solomon 2001). The relationship between spirituality and highly stressful life events is complex, and, in particular, the direction of cause and effect. It seems that whereas some find that stressful events actually strengthen their spiritual beliefs, others find that their spiritual beliefs enhance their ability to cope with stressful events (Connor *et al.* 2003). For example, some researchers have noted that stronger religious beliefs can lead to a greater sense of control, meaning, and deeper intimacy (Tedeschi and Calhoun 1996). It is known that a sense of control in life is very important in relation to resilience in the face of adversity, and that those who experience 'even modest control are more likely to have transformative experiences' (Tedeschi *et al.* 1998, p.226). Sometimes being able to make sense of or to make new meaning of an incomprehensible event can make it more manageable. This can be something that is reached for after a traumatic event, or the inherent sense-making mechanism may already be present prior to a major event happening, such as in the case of having a prior spiritual way of understanding why difficult or painful things happen in life.

Much has been written about what constitutes resilience and how it can be fostered or developed as a protection against life's stresses and traumas. However, there is still little consensus on these matters. Richardson (2002) proposed that resilience is a quality in which an individual possesses strengths or assets that are helpful in supporting that individual during adversity. It is, however, not yet clear exactly what the relationship is between spirituality and its role as a protective factor against developing PTSD. There is some evidence that those who have a spiritual or religious foundation are more likely to experience PTG, but little is known about exactly why this might be the case. For example, in a review of 11 studies that linked religion, spirituality and PTG, Shaw, Joseph and Linley (2005) found that pre-trauma spirituality was frequently found to be beneficial for individuals who were coping with trauma. They also found that traumatic experiences could deepen and strengthen spirituality, and that willingness to engage with existential questions and religious participation were also associated with PTG. For many people with no prior religious or spiritual affiliation, a traumatic life-threatening event can often be a catalyst to searching for meaning in life, by asking questions about faith and the afterlife.

Near-death experiences

A near-death experience (NDE) is a personal experience of imminent death. The most recent *Diagnostic and Statistical Manual of Mental Disorders* (DSM-5) states that among the diagnostic criteria for PTSD there is a specification that the individual has experienced 'exposure to actual or threatened death' (American Psychiatric Association 2013). In the case of near-death experiences (NDEs), clearly this criterion has been encountered. Although not all who experience NDEs develop PTSD, it is nevertheless, by definition, a traumatic event, and some people who experience very distressing NDEs would meet the criteria for a diagnosis of adjustment disorder (Greyson and Evans Bush 1992). There are a number of features typically associated with near-death experiences, including a sense of disconnection from the body, feelings of peace and security, and seeing a light (Sleutjes, Moreira-Almeida and Greyson 2014). These experiences, especially those of disconnection with the body, are often reported as a kind of spiritual experience, even among those with no prior spiritual or religious beliefs.

The repercussions of NDE for those who have experienced them can be quite disruptive, including intra-psychic difficulties such as anger or depression, difficulties reconciling the experience with previous values or religious beliefs, or fears of becoming mentally unwell. Some of the interpersonal difficulties following an NDE may include feelings of isolation from those who have not experienced anything similar, changes in attitude that now do not fit with the expectations of friends and family, and difficulties communicating the impact and meaning of the experience to others (Greyson 1997). As these encounters are outside the range of what might be considered normal experiences, many people who have NDEs do not feel comfortable talking about them, especially with mental health professionals.

In a study by Moody (2001), many of the participants who had experienced NDEs were fearful of rejection and ridicule from others, with participants reporting statements such as 'I've lived with this thing for three years and I haven't told anyone because I don't want them to put the straight jacket on me' and 'After this happened to me, and I tried to tell people, they just automatically labeled me as crazy' (p.86). Because of these anxieties about being labelled as crazy or psychotic, or fearing not being understood or taken seriously, many individuals do not discuss their NDE experiences. However, the spiritual experiences that occur during an NDE are often very important for the individual. For those who are brave enough to share their struggles in counselling or spiritual accompaniment, it is helpful if this spiritual aspect can be a focus of attention in order to assimilate the new experience into their existing meaning structure (Greyson and Harris 1987). Crucially at this point, the therapist's (or accompanier's) response may be the determining factor in whether that individual is able to integrate the trauma for it to provide a stimulus for PTG, or whether it becomes repressed (Greyson and Harris 1987). Repression of certain aspects of experience within the counselling (or spiritual accompaniment) relationship may be harmful for clients, and spiritual issues that the client fears may not be understood or treated with respect and openness may not be shared. It is important, therefore, to maintain an open curiosity about the client's lived experience in all dimensions, including the emergence of their spiritual identity.

Spiritual emergence and spiritual emergency

It has long been acknowledged that there is a clear overlap between what is understood as a spiritual experience and what is seen as evidence of a psychiatric disorder, depending on historical and cultural context. For example, in some cultures people experience spontaneous non-ordinary states that would be perceived as and treated in Western cultures as psychosis. Close observation of these states as they exist in other cultures and spiritual traditions, however, could help us to understand and treat these crises of spiritual opening as processes. In many other cultures beyond Western concepts of the psyche and the soul, the process of 'spiritual awakening' is regarded as a natural process. Many cultures treat this awakening with sacred reverence and have developed rituals to encourage this process of inner growth and transformation (Grof and Grof 1991). Stan Grof (2000) emphasised the role of the unconscious in the course of psycho-spiritual transformation, and has described the two processes of 'spiritual emergence' and 'spiritual emergency' (Grof and Grof 1989). He explains that both 'emergence' and 'emergency' can be triggered by particularly stressful, or traumatic, emotional or physical events that act as a catalyst to the psyche's transformation (Bray 2013). Although the terminology of spiritual emergence and emergency may not be as familiar to those researchers working within the area of PTG, the concepts are familiar. For example, Tedeschi *et al.* (1998) have described a 'more gradual PTG' where rumination, relating to spiritual experiences, is limited, compared with the 'chronic persistence of unabated intrusive rumination' (Calhoun and Tedeschi 1999, p.19). The latter has similar characteristics to the greater intensity described as spiritual emergency.

In the case of spiritual emergence, subtle gradual awareness of spiritual meaning, wholeness and harmony occurs, characterised by a readiness to integrate transpersonal and spiritual experiences, and results in a more mature and expanded consciousness (Grof 2000). Spiritual emergence has been described as a kind of 'birth pang' through which the individual enters into a fuller and deeper life, and into areas of life that were not previously encompassed, by that fullness becoming integrated (Bragdon 1993). However, for some, a trauma can dramatically challenge an individual's psyche, leading instead to a 'spiritual emergency', in which the individual's connection with reality becomes destabilised, causing perceptual problems (Bray 2008). Spiritual emergencies can be disorienting and frightening. They can preoccupy the individual and lead to the performance of private rituals. All of these can present as symptoms of mental disorder. Hallucinations, delusions, anger and interpersonal difficulties are frequent occurrences, and yet these dramatic symptoms can often lead to long-term improvements in overall well-being and functioning (Assagioli 1989).

Especially in Western cultures, this spiritual awakening can occur quite dramatically, whereby frightening but profound insights and unusual perceptions are experienced, producing a kind of personal psychological crisis (Grof and Grof 1991). If supported appropriately, spiritual emergencies offer individuals the opportunity to make changes to values and priorities, and can lead to an expanded worldview, greater personal satisfaction (Lancaster and Palframan 2009) and creativity (Grof and Grof 1991). However, within the framework of current psychiatric understanding, and the chasm between medical and spiritual ways of understanding these experiences, many individuals who are undergoing spiritual crisis are treated as mentally ill and offered psychotropic medication instead of spiritual guidance (Grof and Grof 1991). Although this is potentially more harmful, it has to be recognised that the correct assessment of a spiritual emergency is difficult because these 'non-ordinary' states of consciousness and mental illness cover a wide spectrum of experiences and can occur together (Powell 2005). For example, some clinicians approach addictions as a spiritual crisis rather than a mental health problem (Lukoff 1985). In her work with adolescents, Bragdon (1988) identified several factors that are protective for transformative spiritual emergence, which make this process less likely to turn into a spiritual emergency:

- a conceptual framework that supports, understands and accepts the experience

- the emotional flexibility and structure to integrate the experience (healthy ego structure, tolerance for strong emotions and ambiguity)

- family, friends and social network, including helping professionals, who define the experience as natural, positive, potentially healing or initiatory.

In taking this position, individuals who are experiencing this spiritual transformation could be supported rather than suppressed in order to facilitate healing integration and growth (Grof 2000).

Until recently, there had not been any formal credence paid to the validity of these spiritual experiences. It was not until the early 1990s that Lukoff, Lu and Turner (1995) made a proposal for a new diagnostic category to be included in the fourth edition of the *Diagnostic and Statistical Manual of Mental Disorders* (DSM-IV) (American Psychiatric Association 1994). The new diagnostic category was 'Religious or Spiritual Problem' (DSM-IV, V62.89), and its inclusion marked a change in practice and understanding in psychiatry in relation to professional acceptance of distressing religious and spiritual experiences as non-pathological problems. The diagnosis relates to cognitions and speech, and to themes around spiritual traditions or mythology, an openness to explore the experience, and no conceptual disorganisation

(American Psychiatric Association 1994). This diagnostic category, which is still present in the DSM-5, is used when the clinical focus is a religious or spiritual problem, such as distressing experiences involving loss or questioning of faith, problems related to spiritual conversion, or the questioning of spiritual values that are not necessarily related to any organised religion (American Psychiatric Association 1994, p.685). In the ICD-10 produced by the World Health Organization (1992), a specific diagnostic category does not exist for 'Religious or Spiritual Problem', but it is listed among 'Other specified problems related to psychosocial circumstances'.

There are clearly unique challenges faced by professionals who are seeking to differentiate non-psychopathological religious/spiritual/ transpersonal (R/S/T) experiences from those that might be indicative of psychopathology, especially when one considers the diverse range of these experiences and cultural norms (Johnson and Friedman 2008). Johnson and Friedman (2008) argue that in seeking to identify the differences between spiritual emergence and spiritual emergency, generally, if the individual is displaying excitement, openness and wanting to share that experiences with others, this is most likely to be a spiritual emergence. However, if the experience is significantly hampering the individual's ability to function from day to day, or s/he is finding the experience to be overwhelming, this is more likely to be a spiritual emergency. Powell (2005) has suggested that a further criterion for assessing spiritual emergency is whether the client and therapist deem the spiritual crisis as being something that contains within it an existential truth that is necessary for that individual's future development. Fostering a better understanding of, and honouring, clients' spirituality and how this influences the ways in which they approach their emotional difficulties can assist counsellors, therapists, spiritual accompaniers and other mental health practitioners in distinguishing between growth-related and pathological processes (Peteet, Lu and Narrow 2011).

The spirituality of the counsellor and supporting spiritual emergence

There have been many researchers and authors who have argued not only that issues of spirituality and religion are therapeutically relevant, but also that there is an ethical imperative to consider these matters, especially when operating within culturally diverse client populations

(Young and Young 2014). This is encouraging, as certain emotional difficulties, especially those related to shame and guilt in relation to 'sin', had been seen by some as being solely within the realm of advisors within the faith community (Peteet *et al.* 2011). It is also recognised that there has been an increasing awareness of spiritual matters and willingness for these to be explored within the context of counselling education programmes in relation to the individual client's spiritual journey (Young and Young 2014).

Although it is clear that spiritual matters are important to clients, and are relevant to fully understanding the client's difficulties and the way that they make sense of what has happened to them, often counsellors (unlike spiritual accompaniers) do not fully engage with these issues. Some research has indicated that, as a professional group, counsellors do not see a need to specifically examine their own spiritual values (Bray 2008). Thus, counsellors who have not spent time reflecting on their own spiritual journey, and the similarities or differences of their clients' experiences, may be at a disadvantage in exploring this dimension of a client's world with them. They may struggle to comprehend clients' spiritual questions and dilemmas, and thus find it difficult to help them realise the healing potential of these crises (Robbins, Hong and Jennings 2012). In fact, Fukuyama, Sevig and Soet (2008) argue that in order for a therapist to be able to competently help clients in relation to the spiritual aspects of their lives, they should be able to articulate their own spiritual beliefs and practices, and demonstrate acceptance of their client. However, as Cortright (1997, p.19) suggests, 'in spiritual seeking it is crucial for the therapist to honour all spiritual paths'. No matter what the spiritual position of the counsellor or accompanier, to be most effective in journeying with the client it is essential for the counsellor and spiritual accompanier to have a respectful and humble attitude.

An important intervention for supporting clients to have greater understanding and insight into their experiences is education to help them see their existential struggles as a potentially healing and growing process. In this way, the client is given the resources to manage their painful and confusing thoughts and feelings, and is better equipped to tolerate the process by 'travelling within' rather than attempting to fight against, flee from or suppress it (Cortright 1997). Within the counsellor's, or spiritual accompanier's, competence, an effort to match the client's style to the type of intervention used is also beneficial

(Grof 2000). When clients experience what could be considered to be spiritual or mystical experiences, negative reactions by counselling professionals may increase an individual's feelings of isolation, and may also hinder their openness to seek help to understand and assimilate their experiences (Greyson and Harris 1987). It is therefore important for counsellors and spiritual accompaniers to focus on the client's experience, and to foster an environment of non-judgemental openness and acceptance.

In person-centred theory (Rogers 1962), as with many other approaches, the therapeutic relationship is central to therapeutic growth, and can be considered to be a shared spiritual experience (Gubi 2015c). In transpersonal psychology, in particular, there is an overt recognition that the counselling or spiritual accompaniment journey is one in which both the counsellor/accompanier and the client set out to explore ways to 'find the sacred in the daily ordinary life in which most people live' (Cortright 1997, p.10). The basic foundations of transpersonal psychology are that the nature of human beings is essentially spiritual, having natural urges towards finding wholeness through spirituality, and that consciousness is multidimensional, with spiritual experiences often precipitating experiences at different levels of consciousness (Cortright 1997). These tenets are those that, whatever theoretical tradition one starts from, can be valuable heuristics to align with when dealing with the existential crisis that can often be precipitated by traumatic events. In particular, this approach takes the position that the client is not 'other', but that the client and therapist/accompanier, together, are evolving, seeking and growing (Cortright 1997).

One of the important considerations with regard to entering this collaborative place of healing is that during spiritual emergence and emergency there is a temporary submergence of the client's ego. This allows for an opening towards 'non-ordinary' material and is referred to as a 'holotropic' (moving towards wholeness) phenomenon (Grof and Grof 1991). During the process of coming to terms with this altering state, a fear of losing control is often activated (Bray 2008) and so, ultimately, the benefits of going through this spiritual transition will depend upon the person's ego being able to accept and integrate the outcome of the trauma (Bray 2008). The therapist's/accompanier's role is helping clients to learn what meaning these experiences have for them, and to be sensitive to, and acknowledge, the growth potential in such extraordinary experiences without judging the reported phenomena (Connor *et al.* 2003).

The spiritually competent counsellor

In many cultures, there are not the same boundaries between the psychological, physical and spiritual, and seeing visions or hearing voices are accepted as everyday occurrences (Ankrah 2002). Historically in Western culture, however, the domains of spirituality and religion have been clearly separated from the counselling process. In 1990, a study revealed that although 77 per cent of therapists stated that they tried to align their personal lives with their spiritual beliefs, only 29 per cent felt that spiritual issues were of any importance in their client work (Bergin and Jenson 1990). It has even been the case that many counsellors would be hesitant to discuss clients' spiritual concerns, as this may be viewed as inappropriately encroaching upon the domain of the clergy (Young and Young 2014). As Allen Bergin (1980, p.95) wrote several decades ago, 'psychologists' understanding and support of cultural diversity has been exemplary with respect to race, gender, and ethnicity, but the profession's tolerance and empathy has not adequately reached the religious client'. Unfortunately, this statement still seems as true today in the professional mental health services offered to clients.

Although some clients report that their counsellors are supportive and sympathetic, often clients do not mention certain spiritual experiences to their counsellors due to fears that they will be labelled as mentally ill (Ankrah 2002). Surveys carried out in the United States consistently indicate a 'religiosity gap', with the general public reporting themselves to be more religious than mental health professionals (APA Committee on Religion and Psychiatry 1990). It is unknown to what extent this pattern applies to other nations. Nevertheless, it is clear that there may be a gap between what is usual in terms of the spiritual experiences of individuals seeking support from mental health professionals and the experiences of those people from whom they are seeking support. This prevalence, coupled with what has in the West amounted to a systematic pathologisation, or dismissal, of religion and spirituality, has created a professional insensitivity towards individuals who are presenting with spiritual challenges (Lukoff, Lu and Yang 2011). This demonstrates that although counsellors and therapists are in a unique position to potentially support and help individuals to explore spiritual issues, a lack of willingness to engage in these topics may result in denying clients that opportunity (Fisher 2006). It is to be hoped that this is not the case within spiritual accompaniment.

In counselling generally, there been little training for counsellors in how to attend to clients' spiritual struggles. Nevertheless, spiritual matters, especially during times of bereavement (Gubi 2015d) can often form a significant part of a client's narrative. For those involved in bereavement counselling, engagement with the spiritual domain is a fundamental part of their work (Lancaster and Palframan 2009). At these times, it is not uncommon for clients to disclose psycho-spiritual experiences. In fact, a large number of people report spiritual experiences following bereavement, such as premonitions, visions of the deceased, hearing the deceased's voice, or a sense of 'presence'. Research indicates that sensory experiences of someone who is deceased are very common, with reports from between 39 per cent and 90 per cent of participants in numerous studies of grief and mourning (e.g. Klugman 2006). These experiences can be catalysts for PTG with appropriately sensitive narrative exploration. However, where there may be a rigid difference in views between the bereaved person's meaning structures and those of their helpers, this can prove to be unhelpful and counter-productive (Bray 2013). There is an onus, therefore, on mental health practitioners to engage more seriously with the issues of spirituality as clients present them, in order to better assist clients towards health and growth, especially following trauma.

Research indicates that there are different kinds of cognitive processing that occur following a bereavement or trauma; generally speaking, in the early stages of processing the experience, thoughts are predominantly intrusive ruminations, whereas in the latter stages individuals move into a more deliberate cognitive processing (Calhoun and Tedeschi 2014). This is a generalisation, and it is understood that particularly in the early stages of grief there can be an oscillation between intrusive and deliberate thoughts (Bray 2013). Nevertheless, as a counsellor or spiritual accompanier, appreciating the distinction between these two types of cognitive processing is important, so as to understand whether a client is predominantly experiencing 'intrusive' thoughts, which come unbidden into the individual's experience, or whether they are able to reflect deliberately and consciously on events. The reason this is important is that it can become problematic where there is a continuation of automatic or intrusive rumination, as this may prolong distress (Calhoun *et al.* 2010). In contrast, supporting a client towards more deliberate cognitive processes nurtures their understanding and their reconstruction of a functional worldview.

Notably, this latter stage can only be possible when the individual has moved beyond the stage of 'mere survival' (Calhoun and Tedeschi 2014, p.10). In addition to the development of a sense of meaning and purpose in times of extreme stress, these conversations can also serve to open up explorations of spirituality as a means to find comfort (Pargament *et al.* 2006). At the point at which the client is moving out of the initial phase of intrusive rumination, they can be supported to move towards deliberate cognitive processing, by encouraging self-disclosure through writing and talking (Tedeschi and Calhoun 2006). These are both helpful ways to facilitate integration and to create meaning that supports growth.

Part of the process of finding a way to make sense of what has happened following a trauma, tragedy or major loss is to integrate the new experience into the current life narrative. Neimeyer's (1998) theory of meaning reconstruction, in the wake of shattered assumptions, supports the idea that individuals who experience intrusions of a spiritual nature feel a compulsion to examine and make meaning of their experiences through their narratives, in order to incorporate them into their worldview. Klass, Silverman and Nickman (1996) proposed the theory of a 'continuing bond' with what has been lost, which offers a framework that recognises the possibilities of psychic opening and subsequent growth. Thus, willingness to discuss spiritual experiences can offer a pathway for clients to integrate their spiritual processes and experience PTG (Bray 2013).

One of the challenges in discussing spirituality in the context of trauma is that although spirituality can be a significant resource, the search for and preservation of the sacred can also, of itself, be a source of struggle (Pargament *et al.* 2006). It has also been proposed that greater levels of interpersonal struggle within a religious context are correlated with lower self-esteem and higher levels of anxiety (Pargament *et al.* 2003). The different kinds of struggle that can present are interpersonal (e.g. tensions between family, friends and the religious community), intrapersonal (e.g. personal questions, doubts and fears relating to spiritual matters) and divine (e.g. traumatic events that challenge previously held beliefs about God as all-loving) (Pargament *et al.* 2006). Clearly, these three processes are not mutually exclusive, but usually overlap and are interrelated. For example, those individuals who are more aware of their intra-psychic processes, and are able to adapt to the changes occurring between their inner and outer realities, are more likely to experience growth from these challenges (Grof and Grof 1991). Problematically, however, gaps in professionals' skills, coupled with countertransference processes and a general lack of understanding, arguably contribute to restrictions and deficits in the ethical provision of therapeutic services to clients experiencing spiritual difficulties (Lukoff *et al.* 2011). In the words of Robbins *et al.* (2012, p.93), 'more and more people are seeking spiritual experiences and on their journeys are having crises with which many therapists are ill-equipped to deal'.

The following two extracts are taken from a doctoral thesis which investigated the experiences of fundamentalist Christians who chose to leave their faith community and previously held beliefs for a variety of reasons (Ross 2009). Importantly, part of the thesis examined these individuals' help-seeking practices during this spiritual crisis and, in particular, their experiences of speaking to a counsellor:

> Very few counsellors could even grasp what it was like to be a fundamentalist Christian, and how that would impact your life to leave it. I spent a long time trying to explain this, but it never, they'd just kinda look at you like…I wasn't getting through, or they weren't comprehending or something…they didn't seem to have much of a basis for dealing with it. (p.159)

> If I knew that someone was that naïve about Christianity, I wouldn't even talk about it. Why would I try and tell you how much part of my fibre this is? (p.160)

A willingness and preparedness to engage with the client's cultural and spiritual narrative can be extremely helpful in facilitating spiritual emergence. Another example, taken from research investigating the support received by earthquake survivors from social workers deployed to the region from other communities, reinforces this claim. Findings demonstrated that those workers who were flexible and able to adapt their role to engage with the survivors' dominant cultural narratives were the most effective in facilitating and supporting their recovery (Yang and LaMendola 2007). In this particular situation, the earthquake survivors were part of a collectivist culture, and their cultural beliefs were expressed through their spiritual narratives. Inevitably, each person brings with them a very unique blueprint of thought, attitudes, beliefs, cultural traditions and narratives, as well as spiritual notions and experiences. It is, therefore, important for each counsellor, or spiritual accompanier, to constantly engage in reflective practice, both when present with a client and in his or her absence, whether individually or in supervision.

Summary: The potential for vicarious growth in the counsellor

As stated earlier, traumatic events disrupt both an individual's sense of self and their assumptions about the world, often leaving the person struggling with the challenges of managing their emotional distress and engaging in cognitive processing of beliefs, goals and life narratives (Tedeschi and Calhoun 2006). Working through these struggles can help traumatised individuals to regain positive functioning with a more meaningful and coherent view of self and an increased appreciation of life (Bray 2013).

However, it is well known that burnout, compassion fatigue and chronic stress are all potential risks for counsellors and spiritual accompaniers, especially those who work with a number of clients who have experienced acute or chronic trauma. In severe cases, vicarious traumatisation can also be experienced by counsellors or spiritual accompaniers, where their own view of the world, and themselves, may be influenced by listening to a client's narratives. This possibility is one that counsellors and spiritual accompaniers take care to safeguard against, through a range of self-care practices and by engaging in regular honest, supervision.

One of the protective factors for counsellors and spiritual accompaniers that has been found to be effective in guarding against burnout and vicarious trauma is spiritual, or existential, well-being. In a recent study of 89 counsellors and psychotherapists in Australia, researchers found that existential well-being 'buffered the effect of trauma on emotional exhaustion' (Hardiman and Simmonds 2013, p.1044). The researchers also found that those who reported high levels of existential well-being were also better at avoiding emotional exhaustion when working with severely traumatised clients. These results appear to support the idea that spirituality is a component of resilience and can have a valuable part to play in moderating the potential for vicarious trauma and burnout.

Alongside research into the potential negative impact of working with clients who have experienced trauma has been an increasing recognition that there may be positive benefits for some who are indirectly exposed to trauma, such as counsellors, spiritual accompaniers and therapists (see e.g. Brady *et al.* 1999; Eidelson, D'Alessio and Eidelson 2003). There is emerging evidence that PTG can be experienced vicariously by those who work with survivors of trauma (Splevins *et al.* 2010). This experience relates to observable positive changes in the counsellor or spiritual accompanier following vicarious exposure to trauma (Radeke and Mahoney 2000). Arnold *et al.* (2005) even argue that 'the potential benefits of working with trauma survivors may be significantly more powerful and far-reaching than the existing literature's scant focus on positive sequelae would indicate' (p.239).

Thus, the evidence, overall, seems to point towards a double benefit for counsellors and spiritual accompaniers in reflecting on their own existential or spiritual journey: first, that it is a mechanism for engaging more genuinely and deeply with clients who are experiencing spiritual emergence following trauma; and, second, that it provides a way to manage the personal impact of working with highly traumatised clients. By spending time considering personal spirituality as a self-care and self-development practice, there also exists the possibility of sharing the joy of emergence from darkness to light alongside clients through the experience of vicarious PGT.

Chapter 9

Counsellors and Religious Pastoral Carers in Dialogue

William West

Introduction

For the past 30 years or more, I have been interested in the relationship between therapy and religion/spirituality. For my PhD (West 1995, 1997), I explored the relationship between therapy and spiritual healing. From this, my interest in spirituality and therapy deepened. My first piece of post-doctoral research (West 1998a) involved interviewing 18 Quakers, who were also therapists, about the relationship between their faith and their work, including the impact of their faith on their therapeutic practice. I read and wrote a lot about these and other related topics over the following years (e.g. West 2000, 2004), but the questions about how best to support clients in issues that involved their spirituality, and possibly their religious faith, remained.

If my earlier work was partially about resolving issues around me as a practitioner, more recently it has been the client in me who has been raising questions: if I need help around my spirituality and religious faith, who can best work with me? Is it therapists who may well be secular in their views and practice, or religious people offering pastoral care within a faith tradition? I had this uncomfortable feeling that some potential clients were falling in the gaps between the two – a view reinforced by contact with clients and counselling trainees over the years. I was not confident in therapists' openness and understanding of some faith issues, but also I doubted whether people who were offering religious pastoral care had the necessary counselling skills, or the willingness to journey with me, if I was not staying on the 'straight and narrow' path of their own faith tradition.

Out of these questions arose the idea of running focus groups involving people from faith traditions on the one hand and counsellors with an interest in spirituality on the other. It made sense to use a 'goldfish bowl' (Knox 2011) approach in the group, so that one group discussed the issues and the other group listened. The sub-groups then swapped over, and finally an open dialogue occurred involving both groups.

So far I have co-facilitated two such focus groups. The first involved Christian clergy and spiritually minded counsellors; the second involved Buddhists involved in pastoral care and Jungian-minded therapists.

In this chapter, I will briefly list the main themes from each group, followed by a more substantial version of the joint themes from both groups, including a commentary and some discussion points. I am not aiming to present a research report as such – more a reflection on what this research has shown me and my reactions to it. There are reports in print of both groups (West, Biddington and Goss 2014; West and Goss 2016).

First focus group

For the first focus group, held in Manchester in April 2013, my friend, the Reverend Terry Biddington, co-facilitated the group with me, and we put together a list of people to invite, including ministers from a range of religious backgrounds and counsellors whom we knew. Many of the people contacted were keen to attend, but finding a suitable date was a challenge and, inevitably, there were some no-shows on the day. Nonetheless, we had seven participants – a female Anglican minister, a male Catholic priest, a female United Reform minister, a male Orthodox minister and three female counsellors.

This group was a real eye-opener to me. There was a real willingness to listen to one another within each sub-group, and sufficient trust to share real concerns arising from caring work for people within both. Doing a data analysis of the group presented a big challenge to me. The main difficulty was how to reduce what people had said in over two hours of intense group conversation into some main themes (see West *et al.* 2014).

From a thematic analysis of the focus group transcript, seven main themes emerged:

1. clients' issues

2. language

3. the relationship between pastoral care and counselling

4. counsellors' view of spirituality and religion

5. doing pastoral care

6. training issues

7. participants' own journeys.

Second focus group

It seemed important to get away from a purely Christian group of people doing pastoral care, and from just person-centred or integrative counsellors. I took advantage of having two old friends – both Buddhists, and both doing pastoral care, but within differing traditions – who were willing to participate. Dr Phil Goss, a Jungian friend of mine, offered to co-facilitate a focus group in Lancaster in December 2014. We were able to recruit a number of therapists from a Jungian study group that Phil was part of. Once again, there was a depth of openness and sharing within and between both groups on the day.

Again, the focus group transcript was subjected to a thematic analysis – this time with Phil Goss's help – and, again, seven main themes emerged:

1. spirituality, its meaning, developing it and talking about it in therapy

2. what we mean by God, self and other cultural questions

3. doing Buddhist pastoral care

4. Jungian therapy practice

5. comparisons and differences between therapy and pastoral care

6. the practice and its dilemmas including experiencing 'we' space

7. professional identity and spiritual affiliation.

Composite themes

Recently, I sat down with the main themes from both focus groups and, with the transcripts to hand, I produced the following eight composite themes from across both groups (elaborated on below). I include some extracts from the data and a commentary for each theme. The themes were:

1. Spirituality – its meaning, developing it and talking about it

2. What do we mean by God, self and other issues?

3. Doing religious pastoral care

4. Reflection on clients' issues and the challenges involved

5. Comparisons, differences and the relationship between pastoral care and therapy

6. Professional identity and religious and spiritual affiliation

7. Participants' own journey

8. Training issues

1. Spirituality – its meaning, developing it and talking about it

'For me spirituality is about an integrating wholeness, whether some people use God language or not.'

'And the whole thing about spirituality, that word spirituality, what are you going to use instead? We try and find a way of talking about this experience, which there are no words for.'

'The most precious thing should not be reduced to a word or concept.'

'The way of practising Jungian therapy encourages us not be particularly explicit... If there is a numinous moment, if you start talking about it, describe it, you kill it.'

'Words are not needed; I feel an energy, or a sense of things happening in the room.'

'You may not use the word "spirituality", but you could use words like "your spirit" or "your soul" or "your inner self" or whatever, and I find that I have never been rebuffed.'

Defining spirituality is a well-known challenge (see e.g. Elkins *et al.* 1988). It includes the tension between regarding spirituality as a matter-of-fact part of life and as something innately special. Nonetheless, it had deep meaning to people in both focus groups, and clearly had a range of meaning to them and their clients. If we do see counselling and psychotherapy as only about 'talking', rather than also about experiencing and reflecting on experience, then putting spiritual and religious realities into words may well be beyond most, perhaps all, of us. However, in the deep silence that can occur, when words cease to be spoken, spirituality – indeed the divine – may well be experienced as being present. There is plenty written about the healing power of such moments, referred to as 'I/Thou' by Buber (1970), as 'presence' by Rogers (1980) and as 'tenderness' by Thorne (1991).

2. What do we mean by God, self and other issues?

'If we had a Christianity that recognises not only a belief in God, but a rationalist God, a modern God, a transcendent God, this would provide a more fully relevant version of God. We are talking about 18 or 21 different versions of God.'

'We are more than our minds and our body and our feelings. We are two souls on a journey.'

'We're at this extraordinary époque in human history where the East and the West are coming together; it is extraordinary that we have all these practices and traditions available to us at this time.'

'I tend to use the word "more than" rather than "God" or "Spirit" or anything else and just use it in the context of, "We are more than our mind and our body and our feelings".'

This theme, in many ways, reflects the previous one: just how do we talk about God, about our sense of self, and are we truly sharing a mutual understanding of what these words mean? Any attempt to define God, and what God's truth is, has been a focus for much conflict within and between religious groups. It is thus helpful to be aware of the differing meanings attached to the word 'God'; likewise, within the practice of counselling and psychotherapy, it is useful to notice the differences between Ego and Id, real self, transpersonal or Higher Self, and so on. As ever, listening to the client's view helps and remains a key part of therapy.

3. Doing religious pastoral care

'There just isn't the awareness of the supervisory role, or certainly, in terms of the Anglican Church. There's no expectation that parish priests are in a supervisory role for any of the pastoral care that they are giving, and there's no structure that allows it.'

'If people go along a spiritual path, then in the end they are reaching a point on the edge where there isn't the pastoral support.'

'When someone comes for counselling the agenda feels more open in a certain sense that they might bring anything and that I would try to follow that and help them unfold that but when they come – if I'm within my Buddhist context, then there's a sort of prior agreement... that we're working in a certain way together.'

'Spiritual care is helping people to clarify their spirit path and practices.'

'If spiritual traditions are ideal, which they are usually not, then they have a space and a structure that allows people to grow and develop, supports them at each step of the way.'

There were some rich reflections from both the Christian clergy and the Buddhists on the practice of religious pastoral care (not a word that the Buddhists would themselves use) – for example, concerning whether pastoral care had a different and faith-based agenda to the practice of counselling. There were concerns expressed by the clergy about the supervision of such work and, indeed, whether the training in interpersonal skills for ordination was sufficient.

4. Reflection on clients' issues and the challenges involved

'I'm a Christian. I love Jesus. I shouldn't have these issues.'

'So there's a whole host of emotions that as a good Christian you are not allowed to feel.'

There was candid recognition from the ministers who were present at the first focus group of the limitation of some religious practices, and from the counsellors with regard to best counselling practice around spirituality and religion. Clients may well take into counselling the things that go wrong with their faith, and may feel that they have failed, including having emotions that a religious person should not have. These focus groups were not composed of clients and ex-clients, although a number of participants did speak of their own journeys (see theme 7 below). My concern remained that clients' best interests concerning therapy and spirituality/religion were not necessarily being well served. However, given the counselling background that the clergy and Buddhists shared, and the religious and spiritual insights of the counsellors and Jungian-influenced therapists, here were two groups of people who could, and did, work well in this area. The extent to which these groups might be typical of their colleagues is another matter.

5. Comparisons, differences and the relationship between pastoral care and therapy

'Counsellors seemed to be bogged down with boundaries and dos and don'ts, and rules and stuff.'

'I was struck by how the counselling group together, or at least one of them, seemed to reflect on their perception that religion was rule-bound.'

'It feels like all of the things we are saying to me there's no difference between spirituality and counselling.'

'I was very aware when I started person-centred counselling, I had a Eureka [moment] – I said, "This is just like secular Buddhism."'

'I can't have this conversation with my fellow believers. It's difficult to say to a group committed to a faith, "I've got problems with this..." especially if I am not saying I've got problems and can you correct me – that would be different.'

'When people come to either counselling or a spiritual path it's because they want to grow.'

'I do things in Tibetan traditional Buddhism that I don't do in therapy.'

It is interesting to note that people in both the counselling and the pastoral care group can see the other group as rule-bound. Perhaps both groups are, at times, thus, and need to see when this interferes with best practice. The challenge, in whatever context, is: can we support the client on their spiritual journey even if it is very different from our own? Can we be aware of when referring on is appropriate? That means becoming aware of our skills limit, in whatever role we are offering the client. It also means valuing what the other group offers, and being sufficiently in touch with suitable people to refer to. And would it prove so difficult for us to consider jointly working with a client – that is, where the client consults each of us in turn?

6. Professional identity and religious and spiritual affiliation

'Is it OK, in the professional context, to talk about the spiritual dimension?'

'The Jungian dimension has allowed me to be surrounded, during my training, by like-minded people who also have both their own spiritual journey and also their psychotherapy training, and try to make sense of the whole thing.'

There was a contrast between one counsellor in the first group talking about whether the spiritual dimension could be discussed and a Jungian referring to 'an acceptance' during her training of participants, and future clients' spiritual paths.

7. Participants' own journey

'I'm looking for a Christian community where there's no judgementalism – where it is actually an affirmation of the person in front of you.'

'I've kind of always struggled really in terms of where my faith is and counselling and using the term spirituality rather than religion has been, kind of, on the edges and borders there. So I know my experience and the counselling world and that wouldn't necessarily be the accepted norm of how it would be seen; I've been aware of that.'

There was a sense, from a number of group participants, whether counsellors/therapists or those involved in religious pastoral care, of their own continuing spiritual and (for some) religious journey. This brings to mind Wyatt's work from his research into psychodynamic counsellors and religion:

When I am clear about my faith and comfortable with it – whatever it looks like – then that is good. I know what I think. I know what I believe and I know what I do not believe. I know what my values are, or I know that I don't know. Then, when I am like that, I can listen to clients. (Wyatt 2002, p.182)

8. Training issues

'Where I'm thinking in a pastoral role, you are actually in a relationship that's more intense than many people would work in a counselling relationship with this issue; and yet you have no training and you have no supervision.'

'Being a Christian and talking about being a Christian was quite uncomfortable in that [counsellor training] group sometimes.'

'A lot of times my experience of some ministers is they have no people skills.'

It was interesting, in the first focus group, to note how willing each sub-group was able to be in criticising the limitations of the training available to ministers and counsellors. Given the demands of a pastoral role – and, for ministers, this could well involve them in dual roles and relatively unbounded relationships – it is striking how little support and supervision they receive. For counsellors, the quality and quantity of their exposure to the increasingly diverse spiritual and religious beliefs and practices among people in Britain today is troubling (for example, see Jenkins' (2011) research into clients whose spirituality has been denied in counselling).

Discussion

Reflecting on the two groups as a whole, I am struck by the fact that there was a level of awareness of some very relevant issues relating to therapy and faith. Although it is important to acknowledge that members of these groups were not chosen at random, and they clearly had considerable experience of therapy and spirituality, participants voiced some clearly articulated challenges arising out of best practice in both contexts – therapy and religious pastoral care.

I am left with deep concerns about the training and supervision offered for pastoral care, and the lack of what might be called 'fluency' among counsellors and psychotherapists and their supervisors in dealing with spiritual and faith issues that arise with their clients. As Rowan (2005) pointed out, although Jungian and transpersonal therapists will be well equipped for such work, with humanistic or person-centred therapists it was variable, depending on the therapist and their training.

Some of the challenges involved, I surmise, reflected the situation in wider British society of a largely dominant secular culture, within which many people – perhaps a majority – recognise and value spirituality, while a decreasing and aging minority retain an active religious affiliation. Harborne (2012) has suggested that spiritual direction be considered a modality of psychotherapy. This is not something that I totally agree with, but maybe we need a new, all-embracing word to cover, and include, both forms of helping.

The challenges expressed by my participants are not likely to go away, but they could well be managed better, and worked with more effectively, via best practice in training, supervision and continuing professional development for everyone involved in this work.

Conclusion

Undertaking this research has been a real pleasure for me – a process of bringing together aspects of myself that can be in tension. Although there is not a simple resolution of such tension, its exploration and airing does have a beneficial effect. This research process deserves to be taken further. It is time to attract people from the Islamic, Jewish, Hindu, Sikh and other faith traditions to participate (note: for the original focus group we did invite some Islamic and Jewish participants). In-depth interviewing could be conducted with focus group participants, to tease out some of the themes in more detail and depth. Several surveys could also be conducted to see how generalisable these findings might prove.

Contributors

Ruth Bridges, MA, MBACP (Reg.), FHEA, is a Lecturer in Counselling at the University of Cumbria. She is a person-centred counsellor with a deep personal and professional concern for the realms of spirituality, loss and illness. Ruth has been a counsellor at two Macmillan Cancer Centres where she has worked with the dying, the bereaved and those encountering emotional and physical changes caused by illness.

Dr Phil Goss, PhD, UKCP (Reg), FHEA, is Director of Counselling and Psychotherapy courses at the University of Warwick. He is a Jungian analyst in private practice (Member AJA and IAAP). His published books include *Men, Women and Relationships – A Post-Jungian Approach: Gender Electrics and Magic Beans* (Routledge, 2010) and *Jung: A Complete Introduction* (Hodder and Stoughton, 2015).

Revd Professor Peter Madsen Gubi, PhD, ThD, MBACP (Reg. Snr. Accred), FHEA, FRSA, is Professor of Counselling and Spiritual Accompaniment at the University of Chester, where he teaches on the MA in Clinical Counselling, and is PhD/DProf in Counselling and Psychotherapy Studies research lead supervisor for more than 30 doctoral projects. Peter is a BACP Registered Senior Accredited Counsellor, a BACP Senior Accredited Supervisor, a person-centred spiritual accompanier and an APSE Senior Accredited Pastoral Supervisor in private practice. He has written/edited five books which include *Prayer in Counselling and Psychotherapy: Exploring a Hidden Meaningful Dimension* (Jessica Kingsley Publishers, 2008) and *Spiritual Accompaniment and Counselling: Journeying with Psyche and Soul* (Jessica Kingsley Publishers, 2015). He is a Presbyter in the Moravian Church (British Province), serving as Minister of Dukinfield Moravian Church, Cheshire.

Lynette Harborne, MEd, MSc, UKCP (Reg), MBACP (Reg. Snr. Accred), is a psychotherapist, spiritual director, supervisor and trainer. She works in private practice in Buckinghamshire. She is the author of *Psychotherapy and Spiritual Direction: Two Languages, One Voice?* (Karnac, 2012). She is currently a doctoral student with the Cambridge Theological Federation, where she is researching the ethical practice of spiritual direction.

Dr Nikki Kiyimba, PhD, DClinPsy, CPsychol, is a Senior Lecturer in Psychological Trauma at the University of Chester. She has a research interest in post-traumatic growth and is programme leader for the MSc in Therapeutic Practice in Psychological Trauma.

Dr Valda Swinton, DCouns, MA, MBACP (Reg. Accred) is a Senior Lecturer in Counselling at the University of Chester. She has a research interest in the spiritual dimension of counselling and is programme leader for the MA in Clinical Counselling.

Professor William West, PhD, MBACP (Reg. Accred), FBACP, FHEA, is an Honorary Senior Research Fellow at the University of Manchester and Visiting Professor in Counselling at the University of Chester. William supervises PhD research, and has researched and published substantively on spirituality and counselling. William has written/edited six books and 32 academic papers.

Revd Dr R. Jane Williams, PhD, MDiv, is Professor of Clinical and Pastoral Counseling at the Moravian Theological Seminary, Bethlehem, USA, where she is program leader for the MA in Clinical Counseling.

References

Adelbratt, S. and Strang, P. (2000) 'Death anxiety in brain tumour patients and their spouses.' *Palliative Medicine 14*, 499–507.

American Psychiatric Association (1980) *Diagnostic and Statistical Manual of Mental Disorders, Third Edition* (DSM-III). Washington, DC: American Psychiatric Association.

American Psychiatric Association (1994) *Diagnostic and Statistical Manual of Mental Disorders, Fourth Edition* (DSM-IV). Washington, DC: American Psychiatric Association.

American Psychiatric Association (2013) *Diagnostic and Statistical Manual of Mental Disorders, Fifth Edition* (DSM-5). Washington, DC: American Psychiatric Association.

Andrews, B. (2013) 'An Affair of the Heart.' In J. Tann (ed.) *Soul Pain: Priests Reflect on Personal Experiences of Serious and Terminal Illness.* Norwich: Canterbury Press.

Ankrah, L. (2002) 'Spiritual emergency and counselling: An exploratory study.' *Counselling and Psychotherapy Research 2*, 1, 55–60.

APA Committee on Religion and Psychiatry (1990) 'Guidelines regarding possible conflict between psychiatrists' religious commitments and psychiatric practice.' *American Journal of Psychiatry 147*, 542.

Aponte, H.J. and Kissil, K. (2016) *The Person of the Therapist Training Model: Mastering the Use of Self.* New York, NY: Routledge.

Arnold, D., Calhoun, L.G., Tedeschi, R. and Cann, A. (2005) 'Vicarious posttraumatic growth in psychotherapy.' *Journal of Humanistic Psychology 45*, 2, 239–263.

Assagioli, R. (1989) 'Self-realization and Psychological Disturbances.' In S. Grof and C. Grof (eds) *Spiritual Emergency: When Personal Transformation Becomes a Crisis.* Los Angeles, CA: Tarcher.

Assagioli, R. (1991) *Transpersonal Development.* London: Crucible Books.

Astley, J. (2013) 'The Analysis, Investigation and Application of Ordinary Theology.' In J. Astley and L.J. Francis (eds) *Exploring Ordinary Theology: Everyday Christian Believing and the Church.* Farnham: Ashgate Publishing.

Attig, T. (1996) *How We Grieve: Relearning the World.* New York, NY: Oxford University Press.

Axelsson, L., Randers, I., Lundh Hagelin, C., Jacobson, S.H. and Klang, B. (2012) 'Thoughts on death and dying when living with haemodialysis approaching end of life.' *Journal of Clinical Nursing 21*, 2149–2159.

BACP (2016) *Ethical Framework for Good Practice in the Counselling Professions.* Rugby: British Association for Counselling and Psychotherapy.

Barbezat, D. and Bergman, C. (2014) 'Introduction to the first issue.' *Journal of Contemplative Inquiry 1*, viii.

Barbezat, D. and Bush, M. (2014) *Contemplative Practices in Higher Education: Powerful Methods to Transform Teaching and Learning.* San Francisco, CA: Jossey-Bass.

Barbezat, D. and Pingree, A. (2012) 'Contemplative Pedagogy: The Special Role of Teaching and Learning Centers.' In J.E. Grocia and L. Cruz Castro (eds) *To Improve the Academy: Resources for Faculty, Instructional, and Organizational Development.* Hoboken, NJ: John Wiley.

Barrett, J. (2010) 'Living the Practice: A Research Inquiry into Clergy Use of Reflective Practice Groups in the Exeter Diocese of the Church of England.' Unpublished MA dissertation, University of Middlesex.

Bazzano, M. (2009) 'The teachings of solitude.' *Therapy Today 20*, 1, 34–35.

Bazzano, M. (2013) 'Togetherness: Intersubjectivity revisited.' *Person-Centered and Experiential Psychotherapies 13*, 3, 203–216.

Benner, D.G. (2002) *Sacred Companions: The Gift of Spiritual Friendship and Direction.* Downers Grove, IL: InterVarsity Press.

Benson, J.R. (1987) *Working More Creatively in Groups.* London: Routledge.

Bergin, A. (1980) 'Psychotherapy and religious values.' *American Psychologist 48*, 95–105.

Bergin, A. and Jenson, J.P. (1990) 'Religiosity of psychotherapists: A national survey.' *Psychotherapy 27*, 3–7.

Boisen, A.T. (2005) 'The Living Human Document.' In R.C. Dykstra (ed.) *Images of Pastoral Care: Classic Readings.* St Louis, MO: Chalice Press.

Bonwitt, G. (2008) 'The seam between life and death and therapeutic presence.' *The American Journal of Psychoanalysis 68*, 219–236.

Brady, J.L., Guy, J.A., Poelstra, P.L. and Brokaw, B.F. (1999) 'Vicarious traumatization, spirituality, and the treatment of sexual abuse survivors: A national survey of women psychotherapists.' *Professional Psychotherapy Research and Practice 30*, 4, 386–393.

Bragdon, E. (1988) *A Sourcebook for Helping People in Spiritual Emergency.* Aptos, CA: Lightening Up Press.

Bragdon, E. (1993) *A Sourcebook for Helping People with Spiritual Problems.* Aptos, CA: Lightening Up Press.

Bray, P. (2008) 'Counselling adolescents when "spiritual emergence" becomes "spiritual emergency".' *New Zealand Journal of Counselling 28*, 1, 24–40.

Bray, P. (2010) 'A broader framework for exploring the influence of spiritual experience in the wake of stressful life events: Examining connections between posttraumatic growth and psycho-spiritual transformation.' *Mental Health, Religion and Culture 13*, 3, 293–308.

Bray, P. (2013) 'Bereavement and transformation: A psycho-spiritual and post-traumatic growth perspective.' *Journal of Religion and Health 52*, 3, 890–903.

Bridges, R. (2015) 'The Spirituality of Pain and Suffering.' In P.M. Gubi (ed.) *Spiritual Accompaniment and Counselling: Journeying with Psyche and Soul.* London: Jessica Kingsley Publishers.

Bright, R. (2000) *Grief and Powerlessness: Helping People Regain Control of Their Lives.* London: Jessica Kingsley Publishers.

Browne, A. and Finkelhor, D. (1986) 'Impact of child sexual abuse: A review of the research.' *Psychological Bulletin 99*, 1, 66–77.

Broyard, A. (1992) *Intoxicated by My Illness: And Other Writings on Life and Death.* New York, NY: Fawcett Columbine.

Brunello, N., Davidson, J., Deahl, M., Kassler, R.C. *et al.* (2001) 'Posttraumatic stress disorder: Diagnosis and epidemiology, comorbidity and social consequences, biology and treatment.' *Neuropsychobiology 43*, 3, 150–162.

Buber, M. (1970) *I and Thou.* London: Bloomsbury Academic.

Bunton, P. (2001) *Cell Groups and House Churches: What History Teaches Us*. Lititz, PA: House to House Publications.

Calhoun, L.G. and Tedeschi, R.G. (eds) (1999) *Facilitating Posttraumatic Growth: A Clinician's Guide*. London: Routledge.

Calhoun, L. and Tedeschi, R. (eds) (2006) *Handbook of Posttraumatic Growth: Research and Practice*. London: Lawrence Erlbaum Associates.

Calhoun, L.D. and Tedeschi, R.G. (2014) 'The Foundations of Posttraumatic Growth: An Expanded Framework.' In L.G. Calhoun and R.G. Tedeschi (eds) *Handbook of Posttraumatic Growth: Research and Practice (2nd edn)*. New York, NY: Lawrence Erlbaum Associates.

Calhoun, L.G., Cann, A., Tedeschi, R. and McMillan, J. (2000) 'A correlational test of the relationship between posttraumatic growth, religion, and cognitive processing.' *Journal of Traumatic Stress 13*, 521–524.

Calhoun, L., Tedeschi, R., Cann, A. and Hanks, A. (2010) 'Positive outcomes following bereavement: Paths to posttraumatic growth.' *Psychologica Belgica 50*, 1/2, 125–143.

Canda, E.R. (1990) 'An holistic approach to prayer for social work practice.' *Social Thought 16*, 3–13.

Carel, H. (2008) *Illness*. Stocksfield: Acumen Publishing.

Collingwood, C. (2013) 'Looking at the Bronze Serpent.' In J. Tann (ed.) *Soul Pain: Priests Reflect on Personal Experiences of Serious and Terminal Illness*. Norwich: Canterbury Press.

Connor, K.M., Davidson, J.R. and Lee, L.C. (2003) 'Spirituality, resilience, and anger in survivors of violent trauma: A community survey.' *Journal of Traumatic Stress 16*, 5, 487–494.

Cooper-White, P. (2006) 'Shared wisdom: Use of the self in pastoral care and counselling.' *Pastoral Psychology 55*, 233–241.

Corbin, H. (1972) *Mundus Imaginalis: The Imaginary and the Imaginal*. New York, NY: Analytical Psychology Club of New York.

Cortright, B. (1997) *Psychotherapy and Spirit: Theory and Practice in Transpersonal Psychotherapy*. Albany, NY: State University of New York Press.

Coutts, M. (2015) *The Iceberg: A Memoir*. London: Atlantic Books.

Crisp, B. (2007) 'Spirituality and sexual abuse: Issues and dilemmas for survivors.' *Theology and Sexuality 13*, 3, 301–314.

Dailey, T.F. (1997) *Praying with Francis de Sales*. Winona, MN: St Mary's Press.

Davies, O. (2013) *Theology of Transformation: Faith, Freedom, and the Christian Act*. Oxford: Oxford University Press.

De La Mare, B. (2013) 'The Experience of Stroke and the Life of the Spirit.' In J. Tann (ed.) *Soul Pain: Priests Reflect on Personal Experiences of Serious and Terminal Illness*. Norwich: Canterbury Press.

De Sales, F. (1995) *Thy Will Be Done: Letters to Persons in the World*. Manchester, NH: Sophia Institute Press.

Decker, L.R. (1993) 'The role of trauma in spiritual development.' *Journal of Humanistic Psychology 33*, 33–46.

Denov, M.S. (2003) 'To a safe place? Victims of sexual abuse by females and their disclosures to professionals.' *Child Abuse and Neglect 27*, 1, 47–61.

Dobbins, R.D. (2000) 'Psychotherapy with Pentecostal Protestants.' In P.S. Richards and A.E. Bergin (eds) *Handbook of Psychotherapy and Religious Diversity*. Washington, DC: American Psychological Association.

Doehring, C. (2006) *The Practice of Pastoral Care: A Postmodern Approach*. Louisville, KY: Westminster/John Knox.

Donahue, B. and Gowler, C. (2014) 'Small groups: The same yesterday, today and forever.' *Christian Education Journal 11*, 1, 118–133.

Dougherty, R.M. (1995) *Group Spiritual Direction: Community for Discernment.* Mahwah, NJ: Paulist Press.

Dowling Singh, K. (1998) *The Grace in Dying: A Message of Hope, Comfort, and Spiritual Transformation.* New York, NY: Harper Collins Publishers.

Draucker, C.B. and Martsolf, D.S. (2006) *Counselling Survivors of Sexual Abuse (3rd edn).* London: Sage Publications.

Dryden, W. (1992) *Integrative and Eclectic Therapy: A Handbook.* Milton Keynes: Open University Press.

Dryden, W., Horton, I. and Mearns, D. (1995) *Issues in Professional Counselling.* London: Cassell.

Edwards, D., Bush, M., Vega-Frey, J.M., Duerr, M. *et al.* (2011) *The Activist's Ally: Contemplative Tools for Social Change.* Northampton, MA: Center for the Contemplative Mind in Society.

Egli, J. and Wang, W. (2014) 'Factors that fuel small group growth.' *Christian Education Journal 11*, 1, 134–151.

Eidelson, R.J., D'Alessio, G.R. and Eidelson, J.I. (2003) 'The impact of September 11 on psychologists.' *Professional Psychology: Research and Practice 34*, 2, 144.

Elkins, D., Hedstorm, L.J., Hughes, L.L., Leaf, J.A. and Saunders, C. (1988) 'Towards a humanistic-phenomenological spirituality.' *Journal of Humanistic Psychology 28*, 4, 5–18.

Erikson, K.T. (1976) *Everything in Its Path.* New York, NY: Simon and Schuster.

Faull, K. (2011) 'Instructions for body and soul: 18th century Moravian care of the self.' *The Hinge: International Theological Dialog for the Moravian Church 18*, 2, 3–28.

Finkelhor, D. and Browne, A. (1985) 'The traumatic impact of child sexual abuse: A conceptualisation.' *American Orthopsychiatric Association 55*, 4, 530–541.

Finlay, C. (2013) 'A Burden Not to be Borne.' In J. Tann (ed.) *Soul Pain: Priests Reflect on Personal Experiences of Serious and Terminal Illness.* Norwich: Canterbury Press.

Fisher, P.C. (2006) 'The Link between Posttraumatic Growth and Forgiveness: An Intuitive Truth.' In L. Calhoun and R. Tedeschi (eds) *Handbook of Posttraumatic Growth: Research and Practice.* London: Lawrence Erlbaum Associates.

Fleming, D.L. (1996) *Draw Me into Your Friendship: The Spiritual Exercises – A Literal Translation and a Contemporary Reading.* Saint Louis, MO: The Institute of Jesuit Sources.

Foskett, J. and Lynch, G. (2001) 'Pastoral counselling in Britain: An introduction.' *British Journal of Guidance and Counselling 29*, 4, 373–379.

Frank, A.W. (1995) *The Wounded Storyteller: Body, Illness and Ethics.* Chicago, IL: University of Chicago Press.

Freeman, A.J. (1998) *An Ecumenical Theology of the Heart: The Theology of Count Nicholas Ludwig von Zinzendorf.* Bethlehem, PA: The Moravian Church in America.

Freud, S. (1894/2013) *The Neuropsychology of Defence.* Worcestershire: Read Books.

Freud, S. (1961) 'Civilization and its Discontents.' In J. Strachey (trans.) *The Complete Psychological Works of Sigmund Freud: The Future of an Illusion, Civilization and Its Discontents, and Other Works.* London: Hogarth Press.

Friedlander, M.L., Siegel, S.M. and Brenock, K. (1989) 'Parallel processes in counselling and supervision: A case study.' *Journal of Counselling Psychology 37*, 2, 149–157.

Frommer, M.S. (2005) 'Living in the liminal spaces of mortality.' *Psychoanalytic Dialogues 15*, 4, 479–498.

Fukuyama, M.A., Sevig, T.D. and Soet, J. (2008) 'Spirituality in Counseling across Cultures: Many Rivers to the Sea.' In P.B. Pedersen, J.G. Draguns, W.J. Lonner and J.E. Trimble (eds) *Counseling Across Cultures (6th edn)*. Thousand Oaks, CA: Sage Publications.

Gall, T.L. (2006) 'Spirituality and coping with life stress among adult survivors of childhood sexual abuse.' *Child Abuse and Neglect 30*, 829–844.

Gall, T.L., Basque, V., Damasceno-Scott, M. and Vardy, G. (2007) 'Spirituality and the current adjustment of adult survivors of childhood sexual abuse.' *Journal for the Scientific Study of Religion 46*, 1, 101–117.

Gallese, V. (2009) 'Mirror neurons, embodied simulation, and the neural basis of social identification.' *Psychoanalytic Dialogues 19*, 519–536.

Gallese, V. and Goldman, A. (1998) 'Mirror neurons and the simulation theory of mindreading.' *Trends in Cognitive Sciences 2*, 12, 493–501.

Gallagher, T.M. (2009) *Discerning the Will of God*. New York, NY: Crossroads Publishing.

Ganje-Fling, M.A. (2000) 'Effects of childhood sexual abuse on client spiritual well-being.' *Counselling and Values 44*, 2, 84.

Ganje-Fling, M.A. and McCarthy, P. (1996) 'Impact of childhood sexual abuse on client spiritual development: Counselling implications.' *Journal of Counselling and Development 74*, 3, 253–258.

Giallanza, J. (1998) 'Discerning God's will.' *Human Development 19*, 25, 21–25.

Glaser, B.G. and Strauss, A.L. (1965) *Awareness of Dying*. New York, NY: Aldine Publishing Company.

Goss, P. (2015) *Jung: A Complete Introduction*. London: Hodder and Stoughton.

Graf, L. (2012) 'Learning from our past: Ideas for a 21st century choir system.' *The Hinge: International Theological Dialog for the Moravian Church 18*, 3, 2–12.

Granek, L. (2014) 'Mourning sickness: The politicizations of grief.' *Review of General Psychology 18*, 2, 61–68.

Greyson, B. (1997) 'The near-death experience as a focus of clinical attention.' *The Journal of Nervous and Mental Disease 185*, 5, 327–334.

Greyson, B. and Evans Bush, N. (1992) 'Distressing near-death experiences.' *Psychiatry 55*, 1, 95–110.

Greyson, B. and Harris, B. (1987) 'Clinical approaches to the near-death experience.' *Journal of Near-Death Studies 6*, 1, 41–52.

Griffith, M.E. and Griffith, J.L. (2002) 'Addressing spirituality in its clinical complexities: Its potential for healing, its potential for harm.' *Journal of Family Psychotherapy 13*, 1/2, 167–194.

Grof, C. and Grof, S. (1989) *Spiritual Emergency: When Personal Transformation Becomes a Crisis*. Los Angeles. CA: Jeremy P. Tarcher.

Grof, C. and Grof, S. (1991) *The Stormy Search for the Self: A Guide to Personal Growth through Transformational Crises*. Los Angeles, CA: Jeremy P. Tarcher.

Grof, S. (2000) *Psychology of the Future: Lessons from Modern Consciousness Research*. Albany NY: State University of New York Press.

Groves, S. (2012) 'Response to Graf, L. Learning from our past: Ideas for a 21st century choir system.' *The Hinge: International Theological Dialog for the Moravian Church 18*, 3, 17–19.

Gubi, P.M. (2001) 'An exploration of the use of Christian prayer in mainstream counselling.' *British Journal of Guidance and Counselling 29*, 4, 425–434.

Gubi, P.M. (2002) 'Practice behind closed doors: Challenging the taboo of prayer in mainstream counselling culture.' *The Journal of Critical Psychology, Counselling and Psychotherapy 2*, 2, 97–104.

Gubi, P.M. (2004) 'Surveying the extent of, and attitudes towards, the use of prayer as a spiritual intervention among British mainstream counsellors.' *British Journal of Guidance and Counselling 32*, 4, 461–476.

Gubi, P.M. (2007) 'Exploring the supervision experience of some mainstream counsellors who integrate prayer in counselling.' *Counselling and Psychotherapy Research 7*, 2, 114–121.

Gubi, P.M. (2008) *Prayer in Counselling and Psychotherapy: Exploring a Hidden Meaningful Dimension.* London: Jessica Kingsley Publishers.

Gubi, P.M. (2009a) 'Using prayer in counselling: Exploring good practice for Christian counsellors.' *Accord: Journal for the Association of Christian Counsellors 63*, 14–20.

Gubi, P.M. (2009b) 'A qualitative exploration into how the use of prayer in counselling and psychotherapy might be ethically problematic.' *Counselling and Psychotherapy Research 9*, 2, 114–120.

Gubi, P.M. (2011a) 'A qualitative exploration the similarities and differences between counselling and spiritual accompaniment.' *Practical Theology Journal 4*, 3, 339–358.

Gubi, P.M. (2011b) 'Integrating Prayer in Counselling.' In W. West (ed.) *Exploring Therapy, Spirituality and Healing.* Basingstoke: Palgrave Macmillan.

Gubi, P.M. (2011c) 'An exploration of the impact of small reflexive groups on personal and spiritual development.' *Practical Theology Journal 4*, 1, 49–66.

Gubi, P.M. (2015a) *Spiritual Accompaniment and Counselling: Journeying with Psyche and Soul.* London: Jessica Kingsley Publishers.

Gubi, P.M. (2015b) 'Counselling and Spiritual Accompaniment.' In G. Nolan and W. West (eds) *Exploring Therapy, Culture and Spirituality: Developing Therapeutic Practice.* Basingstoke: Palgrave Macmillan.

Gubi, P.M. (2015c) 'The Importance of Relationship.' In P.M. Gubi (ed.) *Spiritual Accompaniment and Counselling: Journeying with Psyche and Soul.* London: Jessica Kingsley Publishers.

Gubi, P.M. (2015d) 'Accompaniment through Grief.' In P.M. Gubi (ed.) *Spiritual Accompaniment and Counselling: Journeying with Psyche and Soul.* London: Jessica Kingsley Publishers.

Gubi, P.M. (2016a) 'Assessing the perceived value of reflexive groups for supporting clergy in the Church of England.' *Journal of Mental Health, Religion and Culture 19*, 4, 350–361.

Gubi, P.M. (2016b) 'Exploring the Value of (Spiritually) Reflexive Groups in the Training of Ordinands and in Supporting Ordained Persons in Ministry.' Unpublished ThD thesis, University of Winchester.

Gubi, P.M. (2017) 'Embracing reflexivity through spiritually reflexive groups in the training and support of clergy.' *The Hinge: International Theological Dialog for the Moravian Church 22*, 1–40.

Gubi, P.M. and Korris, J. (2015) 'Supporting Church of England clergy through the provision of reflective practice groups.' *Thresholds: The Journal of BACP Spirituality Division*, Winter, 20–24.

Guenther, M. (1993) *Holy Listening: The Art of Spiritual Direction.* London: Darton, Longman and Todd.

Hall, E., Hall, C., Harris, B., Hay, D., Biddulph, M. and Duffy, T. (1999) 'An evaluation of the long-term outcomes of small group work for counsellor development.' *British Journal of Guidance and Counselling 27*, 1, 99–112.

Hall, L. and Lloyd, S. (1993) *Surviving Child Sexual Abuse.* London: Falmer Press.

Harborne, L. (2012) *Psychotherapy and Spiritual Direction: Two Languages, One Voice?* London: Karnac Books.

Harborne, L. (2014) 'Therapy and Spiritual Direction: A Case for a Generic Approach to Supervision.' In M. Paterson and J. Rose (eds) *Enriching Ministry: Pastoral Supervision in Practice.* London: SCM Press.

Harborne, L. (2015) 'The Importance of Supervision.' In P.M. Gubi (ed.) *Spiritual Accompaniment and Counselling: Journeying with Psyche and Soul.* London: Jessica Kingsley Publishers.

Hardiman, P. and Simmonds, J.G. (2013) 'Spiritual well-being, burnout and trauma in counsellors and psychotherapists.' *Mental Health, Religion and Culture 16*, 10, 1044–1055.

Hart, T. (2004) 'Opening the contemplative mind in the classroom.' *Journal of Transformative Education 2*, 1, 28–46.

Hart, T. (2006) 'Pastoral Counseling or Spiritual Direction: What's the Difference?' In N. Wagner (ed.) *Spiritual Direction in Context.* New York, NY: Morehouse Publishing.

Hay, D. (2006) *Something There: The Biology of the Human Spirit.* London: Darton, Longman and Todd.

Heath, L. (2014) 'Keeping our balance: The profound challenge of loss.' *Transactional Analysis Journal 44*, 4, 291–301.

Helminiak, D.A. (1982) 'How is meditation prayer?' *Reviews for Religion 41*, 5, 774–782.

Henry, S. (2011) 'Disfigurement and visible difference: The impact upon personal and personality development and the implications for therapy.' *Person-Centered and Experiential Psychotherapies 10*, 4, 274–285.

Heriot, J. (2010) '"Spiritual but Not Religious": How Small Groups in America Redefine Religion.' In J.F. Maynard, L. Hummel and M.C. Moschella (eds) *Pastoral Bearings: Lived Religion and Pastoral Theology.* New York, NY: Lexington Books.

Heron, J. (1998) *Sacred Science.* Ross-on-Wye: PCCS Books.

Hertz, R. (1997) *Reflexivity and Voice.* Thousand Oaks, CA: Sage.

Hetherton, J. and Beardsall, L. (1988) 'Decisions and attitudes concerning child sexual abuse: Does the gender of the perpetrator make a difference to child protection professionals?' *Child Abuse and Neglect 22*, 12, 1265–1283.

Hinksman, B. (1999) 'Transference and Countertransference in Pastoral Counselling.' In G. Lynch (ed.) *Clinical Counselling in Pastoral Settings.* London: Routledge.

Hockley, J. (2015) 'Intimations of dying: A visible and invisible process.' *Journal of Palliative Care 31*, 3, 166–171.

Holloway, R. (1999) *Godless Morality.* Edinburgh: Canongate Books.

Hughes, G.W. (1985) *God of Surprises.* London: Darton, Longman and Todd.

Janoff-Bulman, R. (2004) 'Posttraumatic growth: Three explanatory models.' *Psychological Inquiry 15*, 1, 30–34.

Janoff-Bulman, R. (2010) *Shattered Assumptions.* New York, NY: Simon and Schuster.

Jenkins, C. (2011) 'When Clients' Spirituality is Denied in Therapy.' In W.S. West (ed.) *Exploring Therapy, Spirituality and Healing.* Basingstoke: Palgrave MacMillan.

Jennings, S. (1998) *Introduction to Dramatherapy: Theatre and Healing – Ariadne's Ball of Thread.* London: Jessica Kingsley Publishers.

Johns, H. (2012) *Personal Development in Counsellor Training (2nd edn).* London: Sage Publications.

Johnson, C. and Friedman, H. (2008) 'Enlightened or delusional? Differentiating religious, spiritual, and transpersonal experiences from psychopathology.' *Journal of Humanistic Psychology 48*, 4, 505–527.

Jones, G.L. (1995) 'The Psychological Captivity of the Church in the United States.' In C.E. Braaten and R.W. Jenson (eds) *Either/Or: The Gospel or Neopaganism.* Grand Rapids, MI: Eerdmans Publishing Company.

Jung, C.G. (1953) *Two Essays on Analytical Psychology*. London: Brunner-Routledge.

Jung, C.G. (1968) The *Archetypes and the Collective Unconscious*. London: Routledge.

Jung, C.G. (1970) *Psychology and Religion*. London: Routledge.

Jung, C.G. (1989) *Memories, Dreams, Reflections*. Toronto: Vintage Books.

Kelly, E. (2014) 'Risking the Embodied Self: A Theology of Presence in Pastoral Supervision.' In M. Paterson and J. Rose (eds) *Enriching Ministry: Pastoral Supervision in Practice*. London: SCM Press.

Kempe, R.S and Kempe, C.H. (1984) *The Common Secret: Sexual Abuse of Children and Adolescents*. New York: W.H. Freeman.

Kerr, P. (2013) 'Snapshots of an Illness.' In J. Tann (ed.) *Soul Pain: Priests Reflect on Personal Experiences of Serious and Terminal Illness*. Norwich: Canterbury Press.

King, M., Speck, P. and Thomas, A. (2001) 'The Royal Free Interview for Spiritual and Religious Beliefs: Development and validation of a self-rated version.' *Psychological Medicine 31*, 1015–1023.

Klass, D., Silverman, P.R. and Nickman, S.L. (1996) *Continuing Bonds*. New York, NY: Routledge.

Klug, R. (2002) *How to Keep a Spiritual Journal*. Minneapolis, MN: Augsburg Press.

Klugman, C.M. (2006) 'Dead men talking: Evidence of post death contact and continuing bonds.' *OMEGA-Journal of Death and Dying 53*, 3, 249–262.

Knox, R. (2011) 'Facilitating a small group teaching session.' *InnovAiT: The RCGP Journal for Associates in Training 4*, 6, 360–367.

Kolb, D.A. (1984) *Experiential Learning: Experience as the Source of Learning and Development*. Englewood Cliffs, NJ: Prentice-Hall.

Kübler-Ross, E. (1969) *On Death and Dying*. New York. NY: The Macmillan Company.

Kushner, H.S. (2007) *When Bad Things Happen to Good People*. New York, NY: Anchor Books.

Lacoboni, M., Molnar-Szakacs, I., Gallese, V., Buccino, G. and Mazziotta, J.C. (2005) 'Grasping the intentions of others with one's own mirror neuron system.' *PLoS Biology 3*, 3, 354.

Lamport, M.A. and Rynsburger, M. (2008) 'All the rage: How small groups are really educating Christian adults. Part 2: Augmenting small group ministry practice – developing small group leadership skills through insights from cognate theoretical disciplines.' *Christian Education Journal 5*, 2, 391–414.

Lancaster, B.L. and Palframan, J.T. (2009) 'Coping with major life events: The role of spirituality and self-transformation.' *Mental Health, Religion and Culture 12*, 3, 257–276.

Lau, J. and Grossman, F.K. (1997) 'Resiliency and adult adaptation in women with and without self-reported histories of childhood sexual abuse.' *Journal of Traumatic Stress 10*, 175–196.

Lawson, R., Drebing, C., Berg, G., Vincellette, A. and Penk, W. (1998) 'The long-term impact of child abuse on religious behaviour and spirituality in men.' *Child Abuse and Neglect 22*, 5, 369–380.

Leech, K. (1994) *Soul Friend: Spiritual Direction in the Modern World*. London: Darton, Longman and Todd.

Lennie, C. (2000) 'The Role of Personal Development Groups in Counsellor Training.' Unpublished MA dissertation, University of Manchester.

Lennie, C. (2007) 'The role of personal development groups in counsellor training: Understanding factors contributing to self-awareness in the personal development group.' *British Journal of Guidance and Counselling 35*, 1, 115–129.

Lewis, A.J. (1962) *Zinzendorf the Ecumenical Pioneer: A Study in the Moravian Contribution to Christian Mission and Unity.* Philadelphia, PA: Westminster Press.

Lieberman, M.A. (1981) 'Analysing Change Mechanisms in Groups.' In B. Bates and A. Goodman (1986) 'The effectiveness of encounter groups.' *British Journal of Guidance and Counselling 14*, 3, 240–250.

Lines, D. (2006) *Spirituality in Counselling and Psychotherapy.* London: Sage Publications.

Lloyd, G. (1983) '"Speaking" in the Moravian Church: An Inquiry into the Historical and Religious Significance of this Practice and Its Implications for Pastoral Care and Counselling.' Unpublished MA thesis, San Francisco Theological Seminary.

Lukoff, D. (1985) 'The diagnosis of mystical experiences with psychotic features.' *Journal of Transpersonal Psychology 17*, 2, 155–181.

Lukoff, D., Lu, F.G. and Turner, R. (1995) 'Cultural considerations in the assessment and treatment of religious and spiritual problems.' *Psychiatric Clinics of North America 18*, 3, 467–485.

Lukoff, D., Lu, F.G., and Yang, C.P. (2011) 'DSM-IV Religious and Spiritual Problems.' In J.R. Peteet, F.G. Lu and W.E. Narrow (eds) *Religious and Spiritual Issues in Psychiatric Diagnosis: A Research Agenda for DSM-V.* Arlington, VA: American Psychiatric Publishing.

Lyall, D. (2001) *The Integrity of Pastoral Care.* London: SPCK.

Mabry, J.R. (2006) *Faith Styles: Ways People Believe.* New York, NY: Morehouse Publishing.

McCann, I.L, and Pearlman, L.A. (1990) 'Vicarious traumatization: A framework for understanding the psychological effects of working with victims.' *Journal of Traumatic Stress 3*, 1, 131–149.

McCown, D. (2016) 'Being is Relational: Considerations for Using Mindfulness in Clinician–Patient Settings.' In E. Shonin, W. Van Gordon and M.D. Griffiths (eds) *Mindfulness and Buddhist-Derived Approaches in Mental Health and Addiction.* Bern, Switzerland: Springer International Publishing.

McDonald, D. (1999) 'Body language and spirituality.' *Search – A Church of Ireland Journal*, Spring.

McLeod, J. (2009) 'Counselling: A radical vision for the future.' *Therapy Today 20*, 6, 11–15.

McMinn, M.R. (1996) *Psychology, Theology and Spirituality in Christian Counseling.* Wheaton, IL: Tyndale House Publishers.

Magaletta, P.R. and Brawer, P.A. (1998) 'Prayer in psychotherapy: A model for its use, ethical considerations and guidelines for practice.' *Journal of Psychology and Theology 26*, 4, 322–330.

Mathers, D. (2014) *Alchemy and Psychotherapy: Post-Jungian Perspectives.* London: Routledge.

Matthews, R. (2015) 'An analytical psychology view of wholeness in art.' *International Journal of Jungian Studies 7*, 2, 124–138.

Mayne, M. (2006) *The Enduring Melody.* London: Darton, Longman and Todd.

Mearns, D. and Cooper, M. (2005) *Working at Relational Depth in Counselling and Psychotherapy.* London: Sage Publications.

Merton, T. (1953) *The Sign of Jonas.* London: Burns and Oates.

Merton, T. (1960) *Spiritual Direction and Meditation.* Collegeville, MN: Liturgical Press.

Miles, A. and Proeschold-Bell, R.J. (2013) 'Overcoming the challenges of pastoral work? Peer support groups and psychological distress among United Methodist Church clergy.' *Sociology of Religion 74*, 2, 199–226.

Minton, K., Hornsey, M.J., Gillespie, N., Healy, K. and Jetten, J. (2016) 'A social identity approach to understanding responses to child sexual abuse allegations.' *PloS ONE 11*, 4: e0153205.

Moody, R.A. (2001) *Life after Life: The Investigation of a Phenomenon. Survival of Bodily Death.* New York, NY: Random House.

Moon, G.W. and Benner, D.G. (2004) *Spiritual Direction and the Care of Souls.* Downers Grove, IL: InterVarsity Press.

Moon, J. (2004) *A Handbook of Reflective and Experiential Learning: Theory and Practice.* London: Routledge.

Moore, J. and Purton, C. (2006) *Spirituality and Counselling: Experiential and Theoretical Perspectives.* Ross-on-Wye: PCCS Books.

Moore, T. (2010) *Care of the Soul in Medicine.* London: Hay House.

Muldoon, T. (2004) *The Ignatian Workout: Daily Spiritual Exercises for a Healthy Faith.* Chicago, IL: Loyola Press.

Murphy, M. (2013) 'Navigating night country: Self-disclosure, mortality, community.' *Psychoanalytic Dialogues 23,* 72–74.

Murray-Swank, N. and Pargament, K.I. (2005) 'God, where are you? Evaluating a spiritually-integrated intervention for sexual abuse.' *Mental Health, Religion and Culture 8,* 3, 191–203.

Neimeyer, R.A. (1998) *Lessons of Loss: A Guide to Coping.* New York, NY: McGraw-Hill.

Neuman, M. (1988) 'Am I Growing Spiritually? Elements for a Theology of Growth.' In D. Fleming (ed.) *The Christian Ministry of Spiritual Direction.* St Louis, MO: Review for Religious.

Newman, J.H. (1925) *Meditations and Devotions.* London: Longmans, Green & Co.

Nicholson, C., Meyer, J., Flatley, M., Holman, C. and Lowton, K. (2012) 'Living on the margin: Understanding the experience of living and dying with frailty in old age.' *Social Science and Medicine 75,* 1426–1432.

North Hollywood, C.A. (2000) 'Bereavement, grief, and mourning.' *Gestalt Review 4,* 2, 152–168.

NSPCC (2013) *How Safe Are Our Children?* Available at www.nspcc.org.uk/globalassets/ documents/research-reports/how-safe-children-2013-report.pdf (accessed 20 December 2016).

Oaklander, V. (2007) *Windows to Our Children: A Gestalt Therapy Approach.* Gouldsboro, ME: Gestalt Journal Press.

Oliver, G. (2006) 'Holy Bible, Human Bible.' In J. Thompson, S. Pattison and R. Thompson (eds) *Theological Reflection.* London: Darton, Longman and Todd.

O'Mahony, S. (2016) *The Way We Die Now.* London: Head of Zeus.

O'Murchu, D. (1994) 'Spirituality, recovery and transcendental meditation.' *Alcoholism Treatment Quarterly 11,* 1/2, 169–184.

O'Rourke, J.J., Tallman, B.A. and Altmaier, E.M. (2008) 'Measuring post-traumatic changes in spirituality/religiosity.' *Mental Health, Religion and Culture 11,* 7, 719–728.

Oxford Paperback Dictionary (2009) Oxford: Oxford University Press.

Pargament, K.I. (1997) *The Psychology of Religion and Coping.* New York, NY: Guilford Press.

Pargament, K.I. (2007) *Spiritually Integrated Psychotherapy: Understanding and Addressing the Sacred.* New York, NY: Guilford Press.

Pargament, K.I., Desai, K.M. and McConnell, K.M. (2006) 'Spirituality: A Pathway to Posttraumatic Growth or Decline?' In L.G. Calhoun and R.G. Tedeschi (eds) *Handbook of Posttraumatic Growth: Research and Practice.* London: Lawrence Erlbaum Associates.

Pargament, K.I., Murray-Swank, N.A. and Mahoney, A. (2008) 'Problem and solution: The spiritual dimension of clergy sexual abuse and its impact on survivors.' *Journal of Child Sexual Abuse 17,* 3/4, 397–420.

Pargament, K.I., Zinnbauer, B.J., Scott, A.B., Butter, E.M., Zerowin, J. and Stanik, P. (2003) 'Red flags and religious coping: Identifying some religious warning signs among people in crisis.' *Journal of Clinical Psychology 59*, 12, 1335–1348.

Park, C.L., Cohen, L.H. and Murch, R. (1996) 'Assessment and prediction of stress-related growth.' *Journal of Personality 64*, 71–105.

Park, C.L. and Helgeson, V.S. (2006) 'Introduction to the special section: Growth following highly stressful life events – current status and future directions.' *Journal of Consulting and Clinical Psychology 74*, 5, 791.

Pattison, S. (2007) *The Challenge of Practical Theology.* London: Jessica Kingsley Publishers.

Peteet, J.R., Lu, F.G. and Narrow, W.E. (2011) *Religious and Spiritual Issues in Psychiatric Diagnosis: A Research Agenda for DSM-V.* Arlington, VA: American Psychiatric Publication.

Pizer, S.A. (2009) 'Love and existential exposure: Reply to discussions by Sandra Beuchler and Martin Stephen Frommer.' *Psychoanalytic Dialogues 19*, 80–86.

Podmore, C. (1998) *The Moravian Church in England: 1728–1760.* Oxford: Oxford University Press.

Porges, S.W. (2011) *The Polyvagal Theory: Neurophysiological Foundations of Emotions, Attachment, Communication, and Self-Regulation.* New York, NY: W.W. Norton.

Powell, A. (2005) 'Spirituality, healing and the mind.' *Spirituality and Health International 6*, 3, 166–172.

Puhl, L.J. (1997) *The Spiritual Exercises of St Ignatius.* Mumbai: St Paul's Press.

Radeke, J.T. and Mahoney, M.J. (2000) 'Comparing the personal lives of psychotherapists and research psychologists.' *Professional Psychology: Research and Practice 31*, 1, 82.

Ransley, C. and Spy, T. (2004) *Forgiveness and the Healing Process: A Central Therapeutic Concern.* Hove: Brunner-Routledge.

Ravetz, T. (2014) *The Incarnation: Finding Our True Self through Christ.* Edinburgh: Floris Books.

Reader, J. (2008) *Reconstructing Practical Theology: The Impact of Globalisation.* Farnham: Ashgate Publishing.

Rennie, D.L. (1994) 'Clients' deference in psychotherapy.' *Journal of Counseling Psychology 41*, 4, 427–437.

Rennie, D.L. (1998) *Person-Centred Counselling: An Experiential Approach.* London: Sage Publications.

Richards, P.S. and Bergin, A.E. (1997) *A Spiritual Strategy for Counselling and Psychotherapy.* Washington, DC: American Psychological Association.

Richardson, G.E. (2002) 'The metatheory of resilience and resiliency.' *Journal of Clinical Psychology 58*, 307–321.

Robbins, R., Hong, J. and Jennings, A.M. (2012) 'In the pause and listening to the little people: A folk healer's journey.' *The Counseling Psychologist 40*, 1, 93–132.

Robson, M. and Robson, J. (2009) 'Explorations of participants' experiences of a personal development group held as part of a counselling psychology training group: Is it safe here?' *Counselling Psychology Quarterly 21*, 4, 371–382.

Rogers, C.R. (1961) *On Becoming a Person.* Boston, MA: Houghton Mifflin.

Rogers, C.R. (1962) 'Toward Becoming a Fully Functioning Person.' In A.W. Combs (ed.) *Perceiving, Behaving, Becoming: A New Focus for Education.* Washington, DC: Association for Supervision and Curriculum Development, 1962 Yearbook.

Rogers, C.R. (1980) *A Way of Being.* Boston, MA: Houghton Mifflin.

Rogers, C.R. (1986) 'Carl Rogers on the development of the person-centered approach.' *Person-Centered Review 1*, 3, 257–259.

Rogers, N. (1993) *The Creative Connection: Expressive Arts as Healing.* Palo Alto, CA: Science and Behavior Books.

Roiphe, K. (2016) *The Violet Hour: Great Writers at the End.* London: Virago Press.

Rohr, R. (2003) *Everything Belongs: The Gift of Contemplative Prayer.* New York, NY: Crossroad Publishing Company.

Rose, J. (2002) *Sharing Spaces? Prayer and the Counselling Relationship.* London: Darton, Longman and Todd.

Ross, K.H. (2009) 'Losing Faith in Fundamentalist Christianity: An Interpretative Phenomenological Analysis.' Unpublished Doctoral dissertation, University of Toronto.

Rowan, J. (2005) *The Transpersonal: Spirituality in Psychotherapy and Counselling.* London: Routledge.

Roy, D. (2005) 'Late words to a dying man.' *Journal of Palliative Care 21,* 4, 235–237.

Roy, D. (2010) 'Transcendence in care of the dying.' *Journal of Palliative Care 26,* 2, 75–76.

Runcorn, D. (2003) *Choice, Desire and the Will of God.* London: SPCK.

Rynsburger, M. and Lamport, M.A. (2008) 'All the rage: How small groups are really educating Christian adults. Part 1: Assessing small group ministry practice – A review of the literature.' *Christian Education Journal 5,* 1, 116–137.

Rynsburger, M. and Lamport, M.A. (2009) 'All the rage: How small groups are really educating Christian adults. Part 3: Anchoring small group ministry practice – Biblical insights and leadership development.' *Christian Education Journal 6,* 1, 112–125.

Samuels, A., Shorter, B. and Plaut, F. (1986) *A Critical Dictionary of Jungian Analysis.* London: Routledge.

Sanderson, C. (2006) *Counselling Adult Survivors of Child Sexual Abuse (3rd edn).* London: Jessica Kingsley Publishers.

Sanderson, C. (2011) *The Spirit Within: A One in Four Handbook to Aid Recovery from Religious Sexual Abuse Across All Faiths.* London: One in Four

Saunders, C. (2006) *Cicely Saunders: Selected Writings 1958–2004.* Oxford: Oxford University Press.

Schön, D.A. (1984) *The Reflective Practitioner: How Professionals Think in Action.* New York, NY: Basic Books.

Segal, Z.V., Williams, J.M.G. and Teasdale, J.D. (2001) *Mindfulness-based Cognitive Therapy for Depression: A New Approach to Preventing Relapse.* New York, NY: Guilford Press.

Shapiro, D.H. (1980) *Meditation: Self-regulation and Altered States of Consciousness.* Hawthorne, NY: Aldine.

Shaw, A., Joseph, S. and Linley, P.A. (2005) 'Religion, spirituality, and posttraumatic growth: A systematic review.' *Mental Health, Religion and Culture 8,* 1, 1–11.

Shaw, P. (2006) *The Sublime.* Abingdon: Routledge.

Shotter, J. (2012) 'Ontological Social Constructionism in the Context of a Social Ecology: The Importance of Our Living Bodies.' In A. Lock and T. Strong (eds) *Discursive Perspectives in Therapeutic Practice.* Oxford: Oxford University Press.

Sims, M. (2011) 'Theologically reflective practice: A key tool for contemporary ministry.' *Reflective Practice: Formation and Supervision in Ministry 31,* 166–176.

Sleutjes, A., Moreira-Almeida, A. and Greyson, B. (2014) 'Almost 40 years investigating near-death experiences: An overview of mainstream scientific journals.' *The Journal of Nervous and Mental Disease 202,* 11, 833–836.

Smith, R. (2015) *Lessons from the Dying.* Boston, MA: Wisdom Publications.

Sontag, S. (2003) *Regarding the Pain of Others.* London: Penguin Books.

Sperry, L. (2003) 'Integrating spiritual direction functions into the practice of psychotherapy.' *Journal of Psychology and Theology 31,* 1, 3–13.

Splevins, K.A., Cohen, K., Joseph, S., Murray, C. and Bowley, J. (2010) 'Vicarious posttraumatic growth among interpreters.' *Qualitative Health Research 20*, 12, 1705–1719.

Steffen, E. and Coyle, A. (2010) 'Can "sense of presence" experiences in bereavement be conceptualised as spiritual phenomena?' *Mental Health, Religion and Culture 13*, 3, 273–291.

Stevens, A. (1994) *Jung: A Very Short Introduction*. Oxford: Oxford University Press.

Stevens, A. (2005) *The Two Million-Year-Old Self*. College Station, TX: Texas A&M University Press.

Strupp, H.H. (2001) 'Implications of the empirically supported treatment movement for psychoanalysis.' *Psychoanalytic Dialogues 11*, 605–619.

Strupp, H.H. and Hadley, S.W. (1979) 'Specific versus non-specific factors in psychotherapy: A controlled study of outcome.' *Archives of General Psychiatry 36*, 1125–1136.

Sullivan, M.D. and Mason, L.M. (2006) 'Slowly dying from sarcoidosis: A patient's story of hanging on and letting go.' *Journal of Palliative Care 22*, 2, 119–128.

Sweeney, R.J. (1988) 'Discernment in the Spiritual Direction of St. Francis de Sales.' In D. Fleming (ed.) *The Christian Ministry of Spiritual Direction*. St Louis, MO: Review for Religious.

Swinton, J. (2001) *Spirituality and Mental Health Care: Rediscovering a Forgotten Dimension*. London: Jessica Kingsley Publishers.

Tann, J. (2013) *Soul Pain: Priests Reflect on Personal Experiences of Serious and Terminal Illness*. Norwich: Canterbury Press.

Tedeschi, R. and Calhoun, L. (1996) 'The Posttraumatic Growth Inventory: Measuring the positive legacy of trauma.' *Journal of Traumatic Stress 9*, 3, 455–471.

Tedeschi, R. and Calhoun, L. (2006) 'Time of change? The spiritual challenges of bereavement and loss.' *Omega 53*, 1/2, 105–116.

Tedeschi, R., Park, C. and Calhoun, L. (eds) (1998) *Posttraumatic Growth: Positive Changes in the Aftermath of Crisis*. London: Lawrence Erlbaum Associates.

Ten Eyck, C.C.R. (1993) 'Inner Healing Prayer: The Therapist's Perspective.' Unpublished EdD thesis, University of South Dakota.

Tetlow, J.A. (2008) *Making Choices in Christ*. Chicago, IL: Loyola Press.

Thompson, J., Pattison, S. and Thompson, R. (2008) *Theological Reflection*. London: SCM Press.

Thorne, B. (1991) *Person-Centred Counselling: Therapeutic and Spiritual Dimensions*. London: Whurr.

Thorne, B. (1994) Developing a Spiritual Discipline. In Mearns, D. (ed.) *Developing Person-Centred Counselling*. London: Sage Publications.

Thorne, B. (1998) *Person-Centred Counselling and Christian Spirituality: The Secular and the Holy*. London: Whurr.

Thorne, B. (2002) *The Mystical Path of Person-Centred Therapy: Hope beyond Despair*. London: Whurr.

Thorne, B. (2006) 'The Gift and Cost of Being Fully Present.' In J. Moore and C. Purton (eds) *Spirituality and Counselling: Experiential and Theoretical Perspectives*. Ross-on-Wye: PCCS Books.

Thorne, B. (2012) *Counselling and Spiritual Accompaniment: Bridging Faith and Person-Centred Therapy*. Chichester: Wiley-Blackwell.

Toner, J.J. (1982) *A Commentary on St Ignatius' Rules for the Discernment of Spirits: A Guide to the Principles and Practice*. St Louis, MO: Institute of Jesuit Resources.

Toombs, S.K. (2004) 'Living and dying with dignity: Reflections on lived experience.' *Journal of Palliative Care 20*, 3, 193–200.

Tracy, D. (1975) *Blessed Rage for Order*. New York, NY: Seabury Press.

Travis, M. (2008) 'Supporting clergy in postmodern ministry.' *Practical Theology Journal* 1, 1, 95–130.

Turell, S.C. and Thomas, C.R. (2001) 'Where was God? Utilising spirituality with Christian survivors of sexual abuse.' *Women and Therapy 24*, 3/4, 133–147.

Ulanov, A. and Ulanov, B. (1982) *Primary Speech: A Psychology of Prayer*. Atlanta, GA: John Knox Press.

VanZant, J.C. (2010) *Prayer in Counselling: The Practitioner's Handbook*. Bloomington, IL: WestBow Press.

Vieth, V., Tchividjian, B., Walker, D. and Knodel, K. (2012) 'Child abuse and the Church: A call for prevention, treatment and training.' *Journal of Psychology and Theology 40*, 4, 323–335.

Waldfogel, S. and Wolpe, P.R. (1993) 'Using awareness of religious factors to enhance interventions in consultation-liaison psychiatry.' *Hospital Community Psychiatry 44*, 5, 473–477.

Walton, H. (2014) *Writing Methods in Theological Reflection*. London: SCM Press.

Watson, K.M. (2010) 'Forerunners of the early Methodist Band Meeting.' *Methodist Review: A Journal of Wesleyan and Methodist Studies 2*, 1–31.

Waysman, M., Schwarzwald, J. and Solomon, Z. (2001) 'Hardiness: An examination of its relationship with positive and negative long-term changes following trauma.' *Journal of Traumatic Stress 14*, 531–548.

Webster, J.P. (1992) 'Verbal Prayer in Psychotherapy: A Model for Pastoral Counsellors.' Unpublished STD thesis, San Francisco Theological Seminary.

Weinlick, J.R. (2001) *Count Zinzendorf: The Story of His Life and Leadership in the Renewed Moravian Church*. Bethlehem, PA: The Moravian Church in America.

West, W.S. (1995) 'Integrating Psychotherapy and Spiritual Healing.' Unpublished PhD thesis, University of Keele.

West, W.S. (1997) 'Integrating counselling, psychotherapy and healing: An inquiry into counsellors and psychotherapists whose works includes healing.' *British Journal of Guidance and Counselling 25*, 3, 291–312.

West, W.S. (1998a) 'Developing practice in a context for religious faith: A study of psychotherapists who are Quakers.' *British Journal of Guidance and Counselling 26*, 3, 365–375.

West, W.S. (1998b) 'Therapy as a Spiritual Process.' In C. Feltham (ed.) *Witness and Vision of the Therapists*. London: Sage Publications.

West, W.S. (2000) *Psychotherapy and Spirituality: Crossing the Line between Therapy and Religion*. London: Sage Publications.

West, W.S. (2002) 'Being present to our clients' spirituality.' *Journal of Critical Psychology, Counselling and Psychotherapy 2*, 2, 86–93.

West, W.S. (2004) *Spiritual Issues in Therapy: Relating Experience to Practice*. Basingstoke: Palgrave Macmillan.

West, W., Biddington, T. and Goss, P. (2014) 'Counsellors and religious pastoral carers in dialogue: An initial inquiry.' *Thresholds*, Summer, 21–25.

West, W. and Goss, P. (2016) 'Jungian influenced therapists and Buddhists in dialogue.' *British Journal of Guidance and Counselling 44*, 3, 297–305.

Wigg-Stevenson, N. (2013) 'Reflexive theology: A preliminary proposal.' *Practical Matters*, Spring, 6, 1–19.

Wigg-Stevenson, N. (2014) *Ethnographic Theology: An Enquiry into the Production of Theological Knowledge*. New York, NY: Palgrave Macmillan.

Williams, D.I. and Irving, J.A. (1996) 'Personal growth: Rogerian paradoxes.' *British Journal of Guidance and Counselling 24*, 2, 165–172.

Wimberley, E.P. (1990) *Prayer in Pastoral Counselling: Suffering, Healing and Discernment.* Louisville, KY: Westminster/John Knox Press.

Wolfe, D.M. and Kolb, D.A. (1980) 'Career Development, Personal Growth, and Experiential Learning.' In D.A. Kolb, I. Rubin and J. McIntyre (eds) *Organisation Psychology: A Book of Readings.* Upper Saddle River, NJ: Prentice Hall Publishing.

World Health Organization (1992) *The ICD-10 Classification of Mental and Behavioural Disorders: Clinical Descriptions and Diagnostic Guidelines.* Geneva: World Health Organization.

Wyatt, J. (2002) '"Confronting the Almighty God"? A study of how psychodynamic counsellors respond to clients' expressions of religious faith.' *Counselling and Psychotherapy Research 2*, 3, 177–184.

Yalom, I. (2008) *Staring at the Sun: Overcoming the Dread of Death.* London: Piatkus Books.

Yang, L.J. and LaMendola, W. (2007) 'Social work in natural disasters: The case of spirituality and post-traumatic growth.' *Advances in Social Work 8*, 2, 305–316.

Yoder, G. (2011) *Companioning the Dying: A Soulful Guide for Caregivers.* Fort Collins, CO: Companion Press.

Young, C.S. and Young, J.S. (2014) *Integrating Spirituality and Religion into Counselling: A Guide to Competent Practice.* London: John Wiley and Sons.

Young-Eisendrath, P. (2004) *Subject to Change: Jung, Gender and Subjectivity in Psychoanalysis.* Hove: Brunner-Routledge.

Zajonc, A. (2006a) 'Contemplative and transformative pedagogy.' *Kosmos Journal 5*, 1, Fall/Winter.

Zajonc, A. (2006b) 'Love and knowledge: Recovering the heart of learning.' *Teachers College Record 108*, 9, 1742–1759.

Subject Index

Author Index

Made in the USA
Middletown, DE
27 April 2017